The Best of Single Life

Bella DePaulo, Ph. D.

DoubleDoor Books

2014

Also by BELLA DePAULO

Singled Out: How Singles Are Stereotyped, Stigmatized, and Ignored, and Still Live Happily Ever After

Singlism: What It Is, Why It Matters, and How to Stop It

Single with Attitude: Not Your Typical Take on Health and Happiness, Love and Money, Marriage and Friendship

Behind the Door of Deceit: Understanding the Biggest Liars in Our Lives

The Hows and Whys of Lies

When the Truth Hurts: Lying to Be Kind

The Lies We Tell and the Clues We Miss: Professional Papers

Is Anyone Really Good at Detecting Lies? Professional Papers

Friendsight: What Friends Know that Others Don't. Professional Papers

New Directions in Helping: Volume 1

New Directions in Helping: Volume 2

New Directions in Helping: Volume 3

The Psychology of Dexter

To the readers of my "Living Single" blog at Psychology Today,
and my other blogs,

especially those who have been participating so thoughtfully and so
engagingly in the discussions of the posts for all these years.

You are truly the best of single life!

THE BEST OF SINGLE LIFE may be purchased for educational, business, or sales promotional use. For information, contact the author or DoubleDoor Books.

DoubleDoor Books

DePaulo, Bella
    The Best of Single Life

ISBN-13: 978-1502332561

ISBN-10: 1502332566

FIRST EDITION: September 2014
DoubleDoor Books

Printed in the United States of America
10 9 8 7 6 5 4 3 2 1

CONTENTS

VIII Are We Missing Out by Being Single – or Are They?

About the Author

Preface

Americans now spend more years of their adult lives single than married. More and more single people have a refreshing attitude about our single lives – we are embracing all that singlehood has to offer, and not just marking time until we find The One. Some of us are not even interested in "finding someone." We do not look to just one person to fulfill all our wishes and dreams. Maybe our lives include "The Ones," such as circles of friends and family and neighbors and mentors, rather than "The One." Maybe we savor the time we spend alone.

Regardless of whether you see yourself as single for now or single for good (and I do mean "good"), if you are interested in living your single life fully, happily, and unapologetically, *The Best of Single Life* is for you. I have been writing about and researching single life for well over a decade, and practicing it for my entire adult life. *The Best of Single Life* includes popular posts from my "Living Single" blog at Psychology Today (which I have been writing since 2008) and my "Single at Heart" blog at PsychCentral, as well as a few articles that appeared elsewhere. In the collection, I explain why single people are thriving, despite all the media memes and scare stories that suggest the opposite. I point to the many single people who choose to be single and why they find the single life so deeply rewarding. I mock those "why are you single" lists that pathologize single people, and offer some real, positive, empowering reasons why many of us are single.

One of the myths about single people is that we are "missing out." In *The Best of Single Life*, I flip that bit of conventional wisdom, and suggest ways in which it is the people who are *not* single who are missing out. Many articles in the collection describe different components of the good life for single people. To live single is to decide for yourself what constitutes the good life. Do you value solitude, independence, sociability, meaningful work, sexual experiences, the pursuit of your passions, and more, or just some of these things? You get to choose. You get to live the life that is best for you.

I.

Why Singles Are Thriving –
Despite All You've Heard to the Contrary

1.

The 7 Secrets of Blissfully Successful Single People

Why do some single people just glow?
Harvard PhD Bella DePaulo spills their secrets

September 5, 2013 by Bella DePaulo, Ph.D. in YourTango

Producers of shows such as *The Bachelor* don't want you to know this. Peddlers of dating guides try to keep it a secret. Some of my fellow scholars pretend it's not true. Even some of your closest friends might contort their faces into expressions of disbelief if you were to suggest it to them. But it *is* true.

Plenty of single people are leading happy and successful lives.

They are not pining for "The One" or crying into their beer. Instead, they are living their single lives fully, joyfully, and unapologetically — whether they plan to do so for one month, for one year, or for the rest of their lives.

What are the secrets of these happily single people?

I've been studying singles for well over a decade, and I think that the happiest and most fulfilled single people have a strong sense of self. They know themselves and trust themselves. Stuck in a matrimaniacal culture — one that is laden with over-the-top hyping of marriage, weddings, and coupling — they are secure enough to know that they can live meaningful and rewarding single lives if they choose to do so — even if they're open to finding a partner, but just not actively looking.

It can seem so much easier to follow the prescribed path that is supposed to lead to happiness: finding your soulmate as soon as possible and then investing just about all of your time, energy, wishes and dreams into that one person. But what if you decided to forge your own path? What might your life look like then?

Strong, happy, successful single people who resist the relentless matrimania and listen to their own hearts practice these habits:

1. They observe themselves. That's an important step toward knowing yourself. Take, for example, the issue of "finding someone." Do you tell yourself and others that you are interested in finding The One — yet, somehow, take specific steps to do so seems to rank somewhere below cleaning out your sock drawer and deleting old emails? Maybe you just think you should "find someone" because our culture is teeming with such messages, but it's not really what you want to do. Mabe not now. Maybe not ever. Know yourself. Then honor your sense of what kind of life is the best life for you.

2. They decide for themselves who counts as special. Maybe they have one special person in their life, but that person is a close friend or a sibling and not a romantic partner. Or maybe they have a whole convoy of important people in their lives, including friends and relatives, mentors and neighbors.

3. They recognize that not everyone wants to be with another person all the time, no matter how special that person may be.

4. They know that all of us want to spend some time alone and some time with other people, and that the preferred mix of solitude and sociability is different for different people. If they crave plenty of time alone, they give themselves the gift of solitude. If they like lots of time with other people, they create a life filled with togetherness.

4. They know whether they like being self-sufficient. And if they do, they go ahead and deal with things and make decisions, mostly on their own. A study of more than 100 Americans who were over 40 and had been single all their lives found that self-sufficiency was linked to their well-being. The more self-sufficient they were, the less likely they were to experience negative feelings. For married people, it was the opposite: The more they liked dealing with things on their own, the more likely they were to experience negative feelings. Self-sufficiency does not necessarily imply a lack of interest in different perspectives or opinions. Instead, I think it means that after considering whatever input you find valuable, you ultimately make the decision that feels right to you.

5. They realize that some people are single at heart. People who are single at heart live their best lives, their most meaningful lives, and their most authentic lives as single people.

6. Single people who do want to marry are wise about what marriage really means. They do not expect marrying to transform them into something they are not. Studies that have followed the same people over many years of their lives, as they stay single or get married, have produced some remarkable, myth-busting results. For example, 18 long-term studies have shown that getting married does not make people lastingly happier or more satisfied with their lives than they were before. Sometimes there is a honeymoon effect — when you first get married, you feel better about your life than you did before. But that feeling dissipates, and eventually, people feel about the same as they did when they were single. A study of American marriages found that people who had been married more than three years were not any happier, they were not any less depressed, they were not healthier, and they had no higher self-esteem than when they were single.

7. They know what the purveyors of conventional wisdom do not – for many people, single life gets even better with age. By studying the stereotypes of single people, my colleagues and I learned that most of society tends to think that single people are not very happy, and as they get older, they become even more miserable. In fact, though, many single people become more secure about their lives over time, and they are less buffeted about by the opinions of other people. They may not even think all that much about being single; they are too busy living their lives.

2.

Who Wrote the Book of Love? Happy Single People

The love of your life may be a what rather than a who

September 14, 2013 by Bella DePaulo, Ph.D at PsychCentral

If I ask, "Who wrote the book of love," you may just start humming the lyrics from the Monotones. There actually is a book of love – *The World Book of Love*, in fact. The subtitle is, "The knowledge and wisdom of 100 love professors from all around the world."

The book will be published in English eventually, but so far it is only in Dutch. I asked the editor, Leo Bormans, if I could share with you the entry I wrote for the book, called "Happy Singles." This single person is happy he agreed.

Happy Singles

By Bella DePaulo, USA

Here is how my essay was introduced:

"I always loved living single," says Prof. Bella DePaulo "except for all the stereotyping and discrimination (I call that *singlism*) and the over-the-top hyping of marriage, weddings, coupling, and romantic love (*matrimania*)." She has been thoroughly studying love and life of singles. And she didn't find misery at all.

Here's what I wrote:

Because of the ways in which marriage and romantic love are celebrated in the media, and even in some academic writings, I assumed that I was mostly alone in my love of single life. Maybe other people wanted out of single life, but I did not. I'm not single because I haven't found just the right partner or because I have issues. Single life suits me. It is, for me, the most meaningful and productive way to live. I'm single at heart.

Once I began to do research I was amazed at what I found. The beliefs that single people are miserable, lonely, and loveless, and want nothing more than to become unsingle are just myths. Those kinds of claims are grossly exaggerated or just plain wrong. The scientific data do not support them. **One of the reasons that so many single people do so well is that they embrace bold and broad meanings of love**, big enough to encompass so much more than just romantic love. It is not just in their words that single people honor the many important people in their lives. Several surveys have shown that single people are more likely than married people to be there for their siblings, parents, neighbors, and friends.

A favorite example in my collection came from the late Ted Sorensen – husband, father, and renowned speechwriter for U.S. President John F. Kennedy. When the *New York Times* asked, "Was your working relationship with J.F.K. the great love affair of your life?" he replied, "Yes, of course." Sorensen was married, but his fervent embrace of work as a source of love and purpose is a lesson to us all, regardless of our relationship status. In fact, it may be single people who most value work that speaks to their soul. A study of high school students found that those who would stay single into their late 20s already valued meaningful work more than those who would end up married. Nearly a decade later, that had not changed.

The title *Liberty, A Better Husband* comes from the diary of Louisa May Alcott. The author was writing about the single woman of antebellum America, who "envisioned her liberty as both autonomy and affiliation…Her freedom enabled her to commit her life and her capacities to the betterment of her sex, her community, or her kin." For generations of women and men devoted to the cause of social justice, **the meanings of love and passion have always transcended diamond rings and red roses**.

Who is the love of your life? Maybe that love is a "what" rather than a "who." Or maybe your love is big enough for more than just one kind of person. If you open yourself to love in its biggest, broadest meanings, you are likely to live your best and most meaningful life.

3.

Fear Not: The Advantages of People Unafraid to Be Single

They are secure, they have high standards, and they are desirable

October 31, 2013 by Bella DePaulo, Ph.D at PsychCentral

You can probably recognize those people, though if you are reading this, you are probably not one of them. I'm talking about people who are afraid to be single. They are rushing into romantic relationships – and staying in bad ones – because they are so scared of living single.

For the entire history of theorizing about single life and some people's eagerness to escape it, what I just said was merely a guess. But now we know for sure. Stephanie Spielmann and six of her colleagues at the University of Toronto have just developed a "Fear of Being Single Scale" and then conducted a series of studies to see how it matters if you are fearful, vs. fearless, about living single. The title of their journal article says it all: "Settling for Less Out of Fear of Being Single."

The "Fear of Being Single Scale" includes items such as these:

- "I feel anxious when I think about being single forever."

- "It scares me to think there might not be anyone out there for me."

- "If I end up alone in life, I will probably feel that there is something wrong with me."

In their article, the authors focus on people who are scared of single life. In keeping with the theme of this single-at-heart blog, I'm going to flip the script, and zero in on the people who are unafraid of being single, and their great strengths and advantages over those who are running scared.

The first area of strength is *personality*. People who are unafraid of being single are more secure in all sorts of ways: They are less neurotic. They get their feelings hurt less often. They are less sensitive to rejection. They are less lonely and less depressed than the fearful ones, and a bit more open and extraverted. Their self-esteem does not depend on whether their romantic partner (if they have one) is being nice to them.

Some people who are unafraid of being single are undoubtedly single at heart (though that wasn't measured in the research), and they may not have been interested in pursuing romantic relationships. So let's look at the people who are unafraid of being single but are pursuing romantic relationships. Those people do so not because they are running away from single life but because they think that a romantic relationship might add something of value to their lives.

Those people have *standards*. When they are in an unsatisfying romantic relationship, they are more likely to break it off than are people who are afraid of being single. And in any of their romantic relationships, good or bad, they are less likely to feel needy and dependent when it comes to their partner (e.g., "If I couldn't be in this relationship, I would lose an important part of myself").

Show the unafraid online profiles of potential dating partners, and you will see how discriminating they are. They are mostly interested in people who seem caring and responsive and attractive. In contrast, people who are afraid of being single express almost as much interest in the totally self-centered people and as in the others.

In speed-dating events, in which participants took part in about 25 dates lasting 3 minutes each, the people who were afraid of being single wanted to give out their contact information to more of the potential partners than did the people who were unafraid of single life. There they are, settling once again.

But here's the really interesting part about those who are fearful of being single and who settle in so many ways and seem to feel so badly about themselves – they were chosen by other potential partners in the speed dating events just as often as everyone else was! They might feel unworthy, but at least in the speed dating context, other people did not see them that way.

When the authors get to the end of their article, they note something very important – that their research is all about the fear of being single and "does not address the potential rewards of being single that may motivate people to be single." Yes, that research is needed!

Oddly, though, in the paragraph before that, they made an observation that sounds uninformed about the whole range of interests and motivations that human beings have. Having reviewed all of the positive aspects of being unafraid of single life, the authors then wonder whether "taken to an extreme, little concern over being single could be associated with an unwillingness to accommodate or settle for anything but the highest standards in a way that leaves romantic or sexual needs unmet." They add that maybe such single people are avoiding intimacy.

The authors seem to be assuming some universal need for romance; there is no such thing. They also seem to assume that everyone is interested in sex, and that the only way to get sex is to couple-up. They also seem to think that intimacy comes in only one flavor, when we single-at-heart types know that close and meaningful relationships can be had with friends and family and all sorts of relationship partners other than the ones you have sex with.

Aside from that one set of reservations, though, I like this work. It demonstrates something I have been preaching for years – if there were less singlism, then that would obviously be good for the single people who would no longer be stereotyped and stigmatized. Importantly, it would also be enormously beneficial for those people who are interested in coupling, because then they could pursue that interest from a position of strength rather than just running away from a life that they fear.

4.

The Best of Single Life:
Lessons from More than a Decade of Study
and a Lifetime of Experience

Living single, deliberately, can be identity-defining and life-changing

September 24, 2011 by Bella DePaulo, Ph.D. at Psychology Today

I have been studying single life for well over a decade and living it for a lifetime. Here are my best guesses as to what counts as the best things about living single.

1.   To choose to live single is to unpack the "truths" that everyone else takes to be self-evident. Singles who have made that choice are probably living their lives more thoughtfully than many others. They are not simply following the predictable and approved paths. Maybe they even know themselves better than many other people do.

2.   Single people who live their single lives fully and without apology probably are, or have come to be, more resilient than others. They are less daunted by the wagging fingers of friends, family, media, and the matrimania that is everywhere. They are inured to the scolding admonitions that they are on the path to no good.

3.   Singles are on the vanguard of appreciating those aspects of life that are of great value, but rarely recognized as such. For example, many singles are especially likely to understand that:

- Solitude can be just as important as sociability; the particular mix of solitude and sociability that is ideal is not the same for everyone.

- "Relationship" is a very big word, referring to far more than just romantic relationships. Singles often value friends, relatives, mentors, and neighbors.

- The conventional meanings of "having it all" or of "balance" are not the only meanings. Singles define what makes their lives meaningful.

- Beliefs about <u>the most desirable amounts and kinds of sex are not timeless or universal</u>. They have changed over the decades and the centuries and they are different in different places. Singles are less bound by the prevailing sexual "shoulds." Singles may also be less judgmental about different sexual orientations, including <u>GLBT</u>, <u>asexual</u>, <u>polyamorous</u>, and more.

4.   There are untold numbers of single people living secret lives of silent contentment and joy. They *like* their single lives. They don't want to become unsingle. But they dare not say so, because they can anticipate the skepticism that will ensue (e.g., the condescending claim that <u>deep down inside</u>, you know you really want to be coupled) and because they think they are the only ones who feel the way they do. To them, I say: Come out, come out wherever you are. If you are happy and you know it, clap your hands. You will be surprised at how many other single people are clapping with you.

5.

More Than Sex: 11 Meaningful Facts About Single People

The real lives of people who are single

February 7, 2013 by Bella DePaulo, Ph.D. at Psychology Today

In a previous post, I critiqued the recently-released report of the "Singles in America" survey. The report is the third annual attempt of Match.com to perpetuate the myth that what single people care about, more than anything else, is becoming unsingle. The company pretends to don the mantle of science, and gets lots of media attention, so it is important to take the report apart claim by claim, rather than just dismissing it out of hand.

The Huffington Post took the press release from Match.com and turned it into a slide show with the title, 10 things you didn't know about single people. The 10 things included such topics as sexting, sex, more sex, snooping in a partner's Facebook or email account, hiding things online, dating, and more dating.

Real single people live bigger, more interesting, and more meaningful lives than those very circumscribed topics would suggest. So here, in tribute to the real lives of single people, are 10 meaningful things you might want to know about them. Click the links and you can read more about each finding, including appropriate qualifications.

1   Singles value meaningful work, and always have

2   Single people have a more diverse set of confidants than married people do

3   Women who get married get fatter. (Men probably do, too.)

4   Single men have good hearts

5   People who stay single exercise more than married or once-married people do

6   For single people (but not married ones), greater self-sufficiency means fewer negative feelings

7   Married people exchange much *less* help with their parents and parents-in-law combined than single people do with just their parents. It is the single people who are there for mom and dad.

8   Single people are more likely than married people to have regularly looked after someone who was sick or disabled or elderly, for at least three months

9   Single people are "more likely to spend time with friends and neighbors than people who are married, and…more likely to volunteer in civic organizations."

10   You know all those things that supposedly go wrong in the lives of the children of single parents? In each of these examples of presumably bad outcomes, the vast majority of the children of single parents are doing just fine.

11   Think there is a marriage penalty? Actually, it is a singles penalty. Single people are subsidizing the breaks married people get in domains such as taxes, health spending, housing, and Social Security

6.

Men and Women Who Have Always Been Single Are Doing Fine

Lifelong singles have strong psychological resources that serve them well

December 7, 2009 by Bella DePaulo, Ph.D. at Psychology Today

Finally, singles are in the headlines in a positive way! Here are a few of the recent media pronouncements:

1. Over 40 and Never Married? New Research Shows You Are Just Fine

2. Never Married, Over 40, Well-Adjusted

My email inbox is lighting up with links to these stories. The questions people are asking me are, (1) have I read the study? (yes, I read the original in its entirety), and (2) is it a good study?

Before I answer the second question, let me tell you more about the research. The authors (Jamila Bookwala and Erin Fekete) analyzed data from a nationally-representative sample of Americans, the National Survey of Midlife Development. From the dataset, they selected the 105 heterosexual people who were at least 40 years old, had always been single, and were not cohabiting, and compared them to currently married people who were also at least 40 years old.

The always-single and the currently-married participants answered questions about their psychological resources, social resources, and positive and negative feelings. (More on all of those later.)

What's good about the study is that it is based on a nationally representative sample, not just a convenience sample of people the authors know. What's not so good about the study is that it gives the married people an advantage from the beginning. Like the vast majority of other studies that compare people in different marital statuses at one point in time, the married group is comprised NOT of all people who ever got married, but only those who got married and stayed married. The 40-something percent of people who married, hated it, then divorced, are set aside. (In contrast, all of the lifelong singles were included in the single group, whether they wanted to be single or not.) So, as always with all studies like this, if the currently-married group looks better than the always-single group in some way or another, that does NOT mean that if only you get married, you will do better, too.

Even with this advantage given to the married group, the always-single group, in comparison, looks just fine. On some measures, there are no differences at all between the currently-married and the always-single. There are no differences, for example, in the degree to which they feel supported by their friends. (The authors consider that a "social resource." On two other social resource measures, kin support and community integration, the singles score a bit lower, in contrast to the results of other national studies.) There are also no differences in any of the psychological resources. For example, there were no differences in **personal mastery**, which is a can-do attitude - a sense that you can do just about anything you set your mind to. There were also no differences in **self-sufficiency**, which is a matter of wanting to handle things on your own.

The psychological resources of personal mastery and self-sufficiency were more important to the always-single people than to the currently-married. You can see that in the links between having those resources and experiencing positive and negative feelings.

Here's how the psychological resource of **personal mastery** matters more to people who have always been single. For anyone - married or single - the more of a can-do attitude you have, the less you will experience negative feelings. But this is even more true for people who have always been single. In fact, if you look just at the married and single people who are high in personal mastery - that is, they are all especially likely to believe that they can do just about anything they set their minds to - the single people are even less likely to experience negative emotions than the married people are. (But if they are especially low in mastery, they experience more negative emotions.)

The results get even more interesting with regard to the psychological resource of **self-sufficiency**, which is liking to deal with things on your own. For people who have always been single, the more self-sufficient they are, the less likely they are to have negative feelings. But for currently-married people, it is the opposite: The more they like dealing with things on their own, the MORE likely they are to have negative feelings.

My take-away from that is that marriage isn't for everyone, just as living single isn't. I wonder whether those married people who wish they could be handling things on their own, and perhaps feeling more restless and unhappy because of that, would have been happier single. Maybe more productive, too.

7.

Are Single People More Resilient Than Everyone Else?

Why are singles happier and healthier than scientists predicted?

May 8, 2013 by Bella DePaulo, Ph.D. at Psychology Today

To write about single life, and to ground what you write in science – which I try to do – is to be constantly put on the defensive. One headline after another proclaims that single people are life's losers. If only they would marry, the argument goes, they too could partake of the greater health and happiness, sugar and spice and everything nice, that are part of the promised package of married life.

I have been critiquing these claims since I wrote my first academic paper and my first book, SINGLED OUT, on single life. Recently, I was invited to write about singles and mental health for the 2nd edition of the ENCYCLOPEDIA OF MENTAL HEALTH. Once again, I reviewed the relevant research on topics such as suicide, depression, loneliness, physical health, and happiness. And once again, I was struck by how little difference it makes to people's health and well-being to go from being single to being married.

I have described many of those findings here at Living Single, such as the underwhelming results of the 18 long-term studies of the happiness of people who get married, and the unimpressive differences in suicide rates in the best research that can be conducted within the ever-present restraints of doing research on marital status (e.g., you can't randomly assign people to different marital statuses).

The weak or non-existent differences are remarkable for a number of reasons. As I have explained many times before, most research is biased to produce results that look more positive for married people than they really are. Yet all of the cheater techniques still do not succeed in making singles look bad.

Consider, too, all of the ways in which single people are disadvantaged. They are constantly challenged by all of the different components of singlism – the stereotyping, the stigmatizing, the interpersonal exclusion from events organized by the couple, the presumption that there must be something wrong with them, and the discrimination that is written right into so many federal laws. In economic terms alone, single people end up way behind their married counterparts.

The singlism is only the half of it. The flip side of the culture of couples is the matrimania – all of the over-the-top hyping of weddings, couples, and marriage.

The real question, then, is not whether getting married results in lasting improvements to mental health, physical health, or any of the other supposed goodies of psychological life – we already know that the answer to that is no. The more profound question, I think, is how it is that single people – especially those who have always been single – are doing so well when so much is stacked against them.

My best guess is this: SINGLE PEOPLE ARE MORE **resilient** THAN EVERYONE ELSE. As I put it in the subtitle of SINGLED OUT, single people are "*stereotyped, stigmatized, and ignored, and still live happily ever after.*"

I am surely not saying that every single person is more resilient than every married person. I'm not denying that there are single people who are not at all healthy, mentally or physically. I'm just saying that when you look at the preponderance of the evidence, single people fare far better than their objective circumstances would lead us to expect.

Single people – again, especially those who have always been single – are also doing far better than social scientists have predicted. For decades, theorists have been spinning stories about why married people are (supposedly) healthier and happier than single people. They have more social support, we are told. Their spouses connect them to larger networks of people. Couples supposedly have a kind of commitment in their lives that single people lack, and married couples' commitment is reinforced by friends and family members and by the society at large. After all, their commitments are public. Other people can watch them and keep them on track. Within the marriage, the spouses can monitor each other, making sure they eat their vegetables and go to the doctor. What's more, the marital relationship is institutionalized, propped up by legal and religious structures.

Some of the theorizing is true (e.g., married couples are benefited and protected by legal structures in ways that single people are not) and some has already been soundly refuted (e.g., people who get married become less connected to friends, family, and neighbors than they were when they were single).

What is almost totally missing from serious scholarly writings about single life are explanations for why single people do so well. Social scientists have been so intent on telling us about the supposed advantages of marriage and disadvantages of single life that they have too often failed to consider the costs of married life and the rewards of single life.

We hear all about how single people are supposedly at risk for becoming lonely, but little about the creative, intellectual, and emotional potential of solitude. As for the opportunities that single people have to create just the right mix of time alone and time together – well, they get short shrift.

We are told that single people do not have the intimacy that married people find in their partners, but hear only crickets about the genuine attachment relationships that single people have with the most important people in their lives.

Missing from the stacks of journal articles is any sustained attention to the risks of intensive coupling (i.e., of investing all of your emotional and relationship stock into just one person, The One) or to the resilience offered by the networks of friends and family that so many single people maintain.

The voluminous literature on marriage pays scant attention to the psychological reality that one size does not fit all. Not everyone lives their best life as half of a married couple, nor, for that matter, do all single people live their best lives as part of a whole network of significant others. Some really do like a whole lot of time alone.

We hear that married people have each other's backs, but if we want to contemplate the ways in which single people pursue their passions, or seek out work that is meaningful, or live a life that may be fuller or more authentic than it would be if they got married, well, usually we will have to write those scripts ourselves.

So, let's do it. Let's write our own scripts.

8.

Why Aren't Married People Any Happier Than Singles? A Nobel Prize Winner's Answer

What is really significant in your everyday experiences of happiness

December 27, 2011 by Bella DePaulo, Ph.D at PsychCentral

"We draw pleasure and pain from what is happening at the moment, if we attend to it." So says Nobel Prize winner Daniel Kahneman in his recent book, *Thinking, Fast and Slow.*

Some of the research described in *Thinking, Fast and Slow* is based on a "Day Reconstruction Method," in which people relive the experiences of the previous day, and answer questions about their activities during that day. They also name the people they were with during the various activities, and they describe their emotions.

Results showed "no differences in experienced well-being between women who lived with a mate and women who did not." Kahneman believes that the ways in which the two sets of women spend their time explain why neither group was happier than the other:

"Women who have a mate spend less time alone, but also much less time with friends. They spend more time making love, which is wonderful, but also more time doing housework, preparing food, and caring for children, all relatively unpopular activities. And of course, the large amount of time married women spend with their husband is much more pleasant for some than for others. Experienced well-being is on average unaffected by marriage, not because marriage makes no difference to happiness but because it changes some aspects of life for the better and others for the worse."

Kahneman's assumptions about which activities contribute to well-being and which undermine it are based on overall results across all of the participants in his research. So in general, people are less happy when they spend time alone and happier when they are with friends. These conclusions do not address the ways that individuals differ from one another. People who savor their solitude, for example, are more likely to be unhappy when they do NOT have enough time to themselves. Similarly, making love may be wonderful when that's what you want to be doing, with the particular person and in the particular way that you prefer; otherwise, though, not so much.

Thinking, Fast and Slow also includes a discussion of a well-known finding showing that among people who get married and stay married, they become a bit happier around the year of the wedding, then they go back to being about as happy as they were when they were single. (I included the graph and discussed it in detail in Chapter 2 of *Singled Out.*) One interpretation of that finding is that over time, married people adapt to being married. They find it joyful at first, but then it becomes routine.

Kahneman instead suggests that we consider how people answer questions such as "How satisfied are you with your life as a whole?" If you are about to get married, or if you just got married, that will come to mind immediately. The decision to marry, he continues, is typically a voluntary one (at least among the people in the U.S. who participated in the study). Therefore, when they think about their forthcoming or recent wedding, they are thinking happy thoughts. Years later, when they are asked the same question about how satisfied they are with their life as a whole, they may be thinking about lots of other aspects of their life, and not (just) their marriage.

One interesting implication that Kahneman spells out is that even among those people whose forthcoming or recent marriage is salient to them, it won't be salient all the time. In their everyday lives, they will often be focusing on other things, and the fact of being married may not have much to do with their moment-to-moment happiness.

The bottom line in *Thinking, Fast and Slow* is that being married (or living with a mate) is of little significance for people's everyday experiences of well-being. That is especially striking because of something I discussed in detail in *Singled Out* but Kahneman never mentions: When he is discussing people who are married or living with a mate, he is discussing a select group – only those who are currently married or cohabiting. The people who got married (or moved in), had a terrible experience and then got divorced (or moved out), are not in the currently-married group. What if everyone who got married had to stay that way?

Imagine, too, the study that can never be done: Randomly assign people to stay single or get married or get divorced. What would happen to people who are single-at-heart if they got assigned to the marriage condition? I don't think they'd be very happy.

II.

Single Life: We Choose It

9.

Americans Just Want to Be Single?

Between ages 25 and 34, married people are in the minority

September 30, 2010 by Bella DePaulo, Ph.D. at Psychology Today

The Census Bureau just released new data a few days ago, from the 2009 American Community Survey, and once again, the number of single people has grown. The nation is even more single than it was a year ago, and it looks so very different than it did a few decades ago. I'll run through a few key "singles rule" stats in the first section. Then in the second, I'll mention some of the explanations that have been offered in the media. (The NEW YORK TIMES gets the award for the most gratuitous, baseless singles-bashing account of why people stay single.) I bet you can anticipate the explanation that did not appear in any of the stories I read.

I.
SHOW ME THE NUMBERS

In numbers and percentages, more Americans are single

There are now about 106.4 million Americans, 18 and older, who are divorced or widowed or have always been single. That's up from 104 million the year before. The percentage of Americans who are not married is creeping ever closer to that 50% mark. (See the note at the end about exact percentages.)

The WALL STREET JOURNAL puts the 2009 figure for married adults, 18 and older, at 52%. They offer a bit of perspective by noting that in 1960, 72.2% of Americans 18 and older were married.

1-person households continue to outnumber married-with-children households

One of my favorite statistics has been the growth of 1-person households as compared to households comprised of married parents and their children (18 and younger). In 1970, 40.3% of households included mom, dad, and the kids, and only 17.1% were 1-person households. In 2009, as has been true since at least 2000, there are more 1-person households (**27.5**%) than married-with-children households (**20.6**%).

Married-couple households continue to be outnumbered by households without a married couple

Counting all households that include a married couple (regardless of whether the households also include kids) still leaves married couple households in the minority. There are more households that do not include a married couple. This has been true for the past 5 years.

Among young adults (25-34), the number who have always been single exceeds the number who are married

Are you at that age when other people start assuming that you should be married by now - say, between 25 and 34 years old? Surprise! In that age group, you outnumber the people who are married.

II.
WHAT ACCOUNTS FOR THESE TRENDS?

The economy
I've been reading various articles in the media about the demographic trends I just described - especially the decrease in the number of married people - to see what stories are being offered as explanations. The New York Times, the Wall Street Journal, and the Associated Press all mention the economy. Maybe adults are postponing marriage until they feel more secure financially.

Increasing age at first marriage
The 'delay' of marriage has been going on for quite some time. The age at which Americans first marry (among those who do marry) has been rising fairly steadily since 1956. So the economy may be contributing to that trend, but the arrow was already pointing upwards when times were good.

High divorce rate
The divorce rate continues to be high, so that contributes to the large number of single people, too. That was noted in several reports.

Increase in cohabiting
An explanation that seems particularly popular is that we can pin the lower rates of marriage on higher rates of cohabitation. Using a beloved

media impress-you word, the WSJ declared that the number of cohabiting couples has "skyrocketed." The NYT quoted marriage scholar Andrew Cherlin: "It is a mistake to think of all unmarried people as single," he said. "Lots are living with partners."

We can do better than "lots." The 2009 American Community Survey reports (in Table S1101) that 5.2% of the 113.6 million households are comprised of opposite-sex unmarried couples, and 0.5% include same-sex unmarried couples. That would amount to about 5.9 million opposite-sex cohabiting couples and close to .6 million same-sex cohabiting couples, for a total of about 6.5 million.

Because I'm going to declare that I'm unimpressed by these numbers, I first wanted to see if any reports claimed larger numbers of cohabitors. A USA Today story begins with this paragraph:

"Cohabitation in the USA is at an all-time high, with the number of opposite-sex couples living together rising 13% in a year's time, from 6.7 million in 2009 to 7.5 million this year."

I don't see a report of the number of same-sex cohabiting couples in that story, so I'll assume a very high estimate of 1 million. In total, that would be 8.5 million cohabiting couples. I just don't think that's a big number.

Remember, in 2009 there were 113.6 million households. More than 31 million were 1-person households. Sometimes people hear this and say it is not a fair comparison, and I need to double the number for the cohabiting couples since there are two adults per household. Fine. That brings the number up to about 17 million. That's still way short of 31 million. Consider, too, that the 31 million figure does not include all the single people who live with other people (such as children, friends, relatives) but not with a romantic partner.

The most irresponsible explanation

Sadly, the one explanation with no data whatsoever to back it was published in the New York Times. The paper quoted Joel Greiner, who said that economic considerations were not the real issue: "It is more a fear of intimacy and fear of marriage."

Who's Joel Greiner? He's "the director of counseling for the Journey, an interdenominational church in the St. Louis area." Couples in his congregation tell him they are living together while they save money, but he's decided they're just scared. That's right - he is not citing scientific research. He's not even pointing to what the people in his congregation have told him, except to say that he doesn't believe it. This is what the NEW YORK TIMES uses to perpetuate its singlism. Singles are just scared of intimacy. Some guy said so.

The explanation no publication suggested

So let's see, is there any other possible reason why more and more Americans are living single? Has it occurred to any scholars or reporters that it is increasingly possible to live a full, complete, and meaningful life as a single person, and so a growing number of Americans are opting to do so? No! Apparently, the thought never occurred to them.

For that, you'd have to go to, say, someone whose thoughts about single life are not prefabricated. Take David, for example. He sent me one of these stories with a note about the low rate of marriage: "Why can't it be because people simply prefer being single?"

10.

How Many People Choose to Be Single?

Here's why we don't know the real answer

September 23, 2013 by Bella DePaulo, Ph.D. at Psychology Today

How many single people really CHOOSE to be single? That's a question I am asked fairly often, typically by people who are skeptical that even one person would really want to live outside of Married Couples Land.

One way to approach that question is to look at survey data. For example, a 2010 Pew Research Report described the results of a national survey of single people. Asked if they wanted to get married, only 46% said yes, for sure (Taylor, 2010). TWENTY-FIVE (25) PERCENT said no—these are the single people who are CHOOSING to be single. Another 29% said they were not sure.

Among those single people who had been married in the past, even more of them—46%—are choosing to stay single.

What we do not know is how many people would choose to be single if single people were not the targets of stereotyping and discrimination and all of the other forms of singlism. What if society regarded single life as just as valid as any other life? Then how many people who choose to be single?

We may like to think that 21st century citizens of America and of the world are oh-so-sophisticated, but in fact, there are social costs to something as innocuous as saying that you are happy, if you are single, and saying that you CHOOSE to be single.

For example, in a study Wendy Morris and I did (not yet published), we found that when married people say they are happy, other people believe them. But when single people say they are happy, other people do not believe them. They think the single people are exaggerating— they are only saying they are happy, when really they are not.

Those skeptics who want to believe that no one would actually choose to be single come armed with their emotions. Three Israeli researchers (Slonin, Gur-Yaish, & Katz, 2010 conference paper) understood this: They predicted that people would actually be ANGRY at single people who said that they chose to be single. They would judge those single people much more harshly than single people who said they wanted to have a long-term romantic relationship.

That's just what they found. The people in their research expressed more anger toward the single people who said they chose to be single, compared to the ones who said they wanted to be in a romantic relationship.

They also made all sorts of negative judgments about the single people who chose to be single. They said those single people were lonelier, more miserable, less warm, and less sociable than the single people who did not want to be single.

I think there are people who not only choose to be single, but who choose it with enthusiasm. Readers of this blog know how I describe such people (I'm one of them)—they are single at heart. I want the concept to become more familiar. Then more single people will realize that there is an alternative to the hunt for The One—they can live their single lives fully, joyfully, and unapologetically.

11.

Wedding Porn Doesn't Turn Us On: Age at 1st Marriage Has Never Been Higher

Matrimania marches on, but marriage doesn't

January 17, 2010 by Bella DePaulo, Ph.D. at Psychology Today

There's a local television ad that is all about a couple's wedding and their love for each other. Not until the last few seconds do we learn that the ad is for a bakery. I wasn't surprised that matrimania was being used to sell muffins. I keep track of such perversions. At the time I wrote Singled Out, my list of items advertised with wedding porn included "cereal and soft drinks; ice cream, chocolate, and cheese; dentistry, headache medication, eye drops, and body lotion; cars, clothes, shoes, credit cards, and lottery tickets; beer, cigarettes, and wine coolers; hotels, real estate, life insurance, and financial institutions" (from p. 15). Since the book was published, I have a new favorite addition: The bridal theme has also been used to sell motor oil. What was special about the bakery ad, though, was that the baked goods were essentially an afterthought; the ad was all about the marriage.

Over at the NATION magazine, Katha Pollitt offered an important observation: Women aren't buying it. Reviewing the highs and lows for women during the past decade, she noted, "Despite oceans of wedding porn, women's age at first marriage rose over the decade."

Men aren't buying the wedding porn, either. The Census Bureau just released the latest figures for 2009. The median age at which men first marry - now 28.1 years old - is higher than it has ever been since the Census Bureau started recording such data in 1890. ("Median" means that half of the people marry before that age and half after.) Women have also never married later in life than they do now. Their median age at first marriage for 2009 is 25.9, a high they reached in 2008.

Below, I'm showing you the numbers from the turn of every decade from 1890 on. I also included the year at which men and women married at the youngest ages on record (1956 - though the men also married that young in 1959), and the most recent year (2009).

Median Age at First Marriage

YEAR MEN WOMEN

2009 28.1 25.9 (oldest)
2000 26.8 25.1
1990 26.1 23.9
1980 24.7 22.0
1970 23.2 20.8
1960 22.8 20.3
1956 22.5 20.1 (youngest)
1950 22.8 20.3
1940 24.3 21.5
1930 24.3 21.3
1920 24.6 21.2
1910 25.1 21.6
1900 25.9 21.9
1890 26.1 22.0

Notice that the 1950's, a time often believed to be the most "traditional" with regard to marriage, is actually the odd decade out. Americans have never married so young before or after that time.

The rising age at first marriage (among those who do marry) is one of the factors that contributes to my favorite statistic: Americans now spend more years of their adult lives unmarried than married. As I noted in a previous post, it is not just Americans who are spending more years single than they have in the past; the trend has gone global.

12.

The Deep Rewards of a Deeply Single Life

5 profound satisfactions of a deeply single life

April 24, 2014 by Bella DePaulo, Ph.D. at Psychology Today

"I want to be in an exclusive relationship with myself." That's how writer Ann Friedman described her desire, around the age of 30, to put an end to her life of being someone's girlfriend for far too many years.

She chose to spend the next years in a state she called "deep single," in which dating was infrequent and repeat-dating with the same person was even more rare. "Those years were, hands down, the most professionally productive and fulfilling of my life," she tells us in an essay in MARIE CLAIRE.

When people who have never really craved the "deeply single" experience try to imagine the appeal, they often come up with things like, you get to arrange your place the way you want it and eat what you want whenever you want. Those can be perks of living single, especially if you are single and also live alone (not all singles do). Friedman described some of the delights of arranging her place and her things the way she wanted them, and not the way she had settled on with boyfriends. When you make your own home, you get to savor it every day of your life, so the matter is not totally trivial.

Yet what the couple-minded don't fully recognize are the deeper ways in which a deeply single life can be satisfying. Here are some of the more profound satisfactions of deeply single life that Friedman described:

1. She pursued the professional opportunities that were most meaningful to her, whether that meant leaving D.C. or moving to Texas or moving a month later to Los Angeles

2. "With only me to stop me, I was unstoppable."

3. Her social life expanded (consistent with tons of research). Instead of spending all her time with the same social group that she and her boyfriend had ossified in, she nurtured her connections with several circles of friends.

4. She got to spend "a lot of quality time alone." For people who love their single lives, alone time is rarely frightening or even boring; it is more often profoundly satisfying.

5. "Being single doesn't just make you more independent: It makes you more interesting."

Friedman also became a bit less pliant about the "poor-me, I'm-single" conversations that went on around her. She just would not participate in them anymore. Having sampled the deep satisfactions of deeply single life, she found it "excruciating to hear women talk about how desperate they are to be in a relationship—any relationship." Ann Friedman liked truth better than clichés, and the truth she discovered was that "your 'real life' doesn't begin when you meet a partner. It's happening now."

There is something else Friedman mentioned, which grabbed me not because it counts as one of the deepest rewards of single life, but because it is a metaphor for single life that one person after another finds attractive and apt: She and her best friend drove along the coast, "a vacation we'd fantasized about for years." Open road, vast ocean views—something about that says "single" in a fundamentally positive way.

I love how beautifully Friedman articulated the profound appeal of a deeply single life, but I'm not so sure she is single at heart. She talks about those deeply single years as if they are in the past, so perhaps they are. Maybe her experiences suggest something else important about the single-at-heart experience. Maybe it is not just something enduring about a person, like a personality trait. Perhaps for some people, living the deeply single life is something that is tremendously appealing for years, but not for a lifetime. We have so much more to learn about what single-at-heart really means.

13.

Single Life as a 'Satisfying Choice and a Profound Threat'

When spinster was a compliment and single men were not vilified

May 31, 2010 by Bella DePaulo, Ph.D. at Psychology Today

I've always known that Americans are not the most historically-minded. In my high school, history was taught by the football and basketball coaches, and they mostly enlightened us about the history of the game the night before. So when I first started reading about the history of marriage, coupling, and singlehood, I was astounded to discover how different attitudes and practices have been at different times and in different places. Historically speaking, marrying for love is a relatively recent phenomenon, and the kind of intensive coupling Americans often practice (the "you are my everything" variety) is, in the big picture, just weird.

Elizabeth Abbott's book, A History of Marriage, is hardly the first book on the topic. I'm not sure why she wrote it, but I'm glad she did. Of the accounts I've read, Abbott's is the only one to include a chapter on singles.

Why should there be a chapter on singles in a book about marriage? Here's what Abbott says:

> "Whether because of war, vocation, profession, economics, or personal choice, significant minorities of men and even more women have lived as singles, and theirs is a hitherto hidden history of human relations and marriage."

Don't let the "hitherto" fool you. Abbott is a wonderfully engaging storyteller, so even if you are not particularly interested in the history of marriage, you might enjoy this book.

Just how significant have those minorities of single men and women been in the past? "In the eighteenth century," Abbott notes, "about 25 percent of English and 30 percent of Scottish aristocratic women remained single." In my own writing, I like to dig up the latest Census figures and note that the percentage of single men and women has been growing and growing. Typically, though, I'm just looking back four or five decades, or occasionally, a little over a century. That's short-term history. Living single, and staying that way for life, is hardly a contemporary American phenomenon.

But what about our attitudes? Are they unique? Discussing the Civil War, in which at least 618,000 Americans died, Abbott says this: "Back home, as official death notices began to arrive, single women realized that many of them would never find husbands." What do you expect to read right after that sentence?

Here's what actually did follow: "By no means all of them grieved at their fate."

That sort of delightful subversiveness and surprise is sprinkled throughout the book. The introduction, for example, begins with the story of a couple getting married. The bride, in describing the picture of her life together with her husband, says that she sees a huge "sky filled with bubbles and lollipops." Now, if I didn't know there was a chapter on singles coming up, I would have closed the book right then and there. It turned out, though, that this was not a cloyingly matrimaniacal couple. Instead, the twosome had already been together for 14 years. They wanted to adopt, but the adoption agency would only consider officially married couples.

Did you know that the term "spinster" once was a nod to the economic independence of women who could support themselves by spinning wool? Obviously, that changed: "at the same time that contingents of spinsters were enjoying satisfying and fulfilled lives, the cult of domesticity's new sentimentality about wives increasingly recast spinsters as socially inadequate losers."

Abbott mentions this Living Single blog in her book, so I wish I could say that I found nothing to criticize in her writing. Unfortunately, though, there was one point at which I thought the book had been hijacked by some crazed member of the Marriage Mafia. Referring to the battles that are still brewing over custody issues, Abbott says this: "If they are not resolved, generations of children will grow into adulthood at risk of being wounded or stunted, susceptible to depression and social withdrawal." When I titled my chapter in Singled Out on single parent families, "Attention, single parents - your kids are doomed," I was mocking the overblown rhetoric. Abbott's prediction about "stunted" children seemed to be offered in all seriousness.

Maybe that was just an aberration. In the epilogue, where Abbott tells us her own opinions, she says this:

> "I do not believe that marriage is the right way of life for everyone."

> "I believe that divorce is not necessarily a failure, that it may also be a solution or a release."

Finally, I think Abbott nailed the place of singles in contemporary society when she said:

> "The choices and possibilities are now so entrenched in North American society that singleness has become both a satisfying choice and a profound threat to the institution of marriage."

14.

Yes, We Really Do Want Lifelong Singlehood

People who are single-at-heart do want lifelong singlehood

September 10, 2012 by Bella DePaulo, Ph.D. at Psychology Today

Here's the short answer to the question posed by the recent PSYCHOLOGY TODAY post, "Do you really want lifelong singlehood?" Yes.

Yes, we do. We who are *single at heart* love our single lives. To live single is to live our most authentic and meaningful lives. We are not just telling ourselves that, "consciously or unconsciously hiding from the pain of not having the relationship [we] truly want." I wonder whether the authors of the post in question realize, consciously or unconsciously, just how condescending that statement truly is. They, who have never met the vast majority of the single people they are demeaning by their "hiding from the pain" insult, seem to think they know better than the single people themselves.

The authors note that teenagers still say that marriage is very important to them. Teenagers, yes. But what about the Pew surveys of grown-ups? In response to the question, "Do you want to get married," only 46 percent said yes.

Of course, the authors did throw us the sop, "while some may be perfectly happy being single;" yet the rest of the post is a throw-back to the days before there was much consciousness-raising about single life or critical thinking about marriage and matrimania. Now, there are so many bloggers writing in thoughtful ways about single life that there is a website, Single with Attitude, which aggregates their feeds. You won't find those bloggers whining, "Poor me, I'm single!" They are not yearning to become unsingle.

Consider a few choice excerpts from the post questioning whether we really want lifelong singlehood:

- "People stop fixing you up for dates, because they believe you really prefer being single, even if you don't really want to be." (They say this as if it is a bad thing if people stop trying to "fix" you.)

- Hey, relationships aren't easy, but they can help: "So don't give up yet!"

- Then there's this: "Stay tuned – and stay Couple!"

- This next one is almost a self-parody. The authors advise couples to come up with a "couple proclamation" such as "We are one" and recite it every day. As Dave Barry used to say, I swear I'm not making this up. The authors promise that if you say your "We are one" proclamation every day you will have "couple power."

The authors also seem totally oblivious to the embarrassing methodological problems that plague most studies claiming to show the "marked personal and social benefits of marriage over singlehood or cohabitation." I reviewed those scientific embarrassments, and described what really could be concluded from that research, in one chapter after another of *Singled Out*. As more studies have appeared, I have continued to critique them in this Living Single blog that I have been writing since 2008.

I guess the authors also don't know about the many ways in which people who stay single for life do just fine. Maybe they have not considered the possibility that many Americans just want to be single. (They cite the matrimaniacal National Marriage Project in their opening paragraph, so that gives you a hint about where they are coming from.)

So to the authors: If you have single people who come to you in your practice and say they are wondering whether they really do want to be coupled, and would like some help, then have at them. But please do not presume that the people who come to see you in your practice represent all or even most single people. Please do not imply that if only we got married, we would enjoy "marked personal and social benefits." There are many of us who love our single lives, and are tremendously grateful that we live in a time when we don't all have to live a one-size-fits-all life and get married and have children. That was the 1950s. This is the 21st century. Now our wish is for the *singlism* to stop. I think you can help people who want to be coupled without denigrating those who do not. And as PhDs, I think it is particular important that you not make claims about the scientific literature that are exaggerated or just plain false.

15.

Single by Choice: A High-Profile Celebration

A cover story on single people who choose single life

January 4, 2012 by Bella DePaulo, Ph.D at PsychCentral

"THIS IS TERRI. SHE'S SUCCESSFUL, HAPPY, AND AT 38, JUST FINE WITH NEVER GETTING MARRIED. EVER."

That's the caption to the picture illustrating an article I've been fantasizing about for more than a decade. Finally, someone has actually written it. The article is the cover story of the most recent issue of BOSTON MAGAZINE, "Single by choice: Why more of us than ever before are happy to never get married."

Reporter Janelle Nanos nails it about what living single means to those who CHOOSE that life. She debunks stereotypes, highlights all the matrimania and singlism, and shows how and why there are more and more people living their single lives fully, joyfully, and without apology.

How's this for a story of astounding singlism in the workplace? It is from Eva, who works in finance in Boston, and whose boss recently presented Christmas gifts to his employees:

> "After he handed out a bottle of wine to every other employee in her department, Eva unwrapped a small bar of soap with a cat sticker on it, and an accompanying mug that said, 'Everything Tastes Better with Cat Hair in It.'"

Probably my favorite quote in the story is about Trish, a 74-year old who has always been single:

> "She's been in long-term relationships, and once thought about getting married, but decided to go to Nigeria instead."

Readers of this "Single at Heart" blog may be especially interested to know that Janelle Nanos describes the "single at heart" concept in her story. She also mentions the *Singled Out* and *Singlism* books. She credits the Alternatives to Marriage Project for their important advocacy work, and points to findings from the Sloan Work and Family Research Network about singles in the workplace.

The Boston Magazine story underscores the significant demographic facts – single people, and 1-person households, are on the rise. Then, rather than taking the usual turn of tut-tutting that outcome, Nanos points to Pew project data showing the large percentage of people who WANT to be single.

Nanos interviews modern-day spinsters – really, women who spin – who are proud of their passions, and she lets us in on a wonderful historical nugget: Originally, "spinster" was a term of honor. It referred to women who supported themselves by spinning wool and "were celebrated for their unwillingness to compromise their moral standards for the sake of a relationship."

Read the story, and you will get a sneak preview of some important, soon-to-be-published books that will continue the theme of the strengths and social connections and joys of people who are single.

16.

The Allure of Single Life

What different singles love about their single lives

November 7, 2011 by Bella DePaulo, Ph.D at PsychCentral

"Sometimes I want to be single." That's what a reader wrote to the author of a "Love Letters" column, in an exchange that drew a huge response (for example, more than 1100 comments and a special segment on Boston's NPR station). What so many people found intriguing about this reader who wondered whether single life suited her best was that she was in a long-term relationship with a person she described as

> "an amazing, wonderful man. We have a fantastic relationship. Communicate well. When he kisses me, I still get goose bumps. When he walks into the room, I am always mesmerized by him."

But here's the rub:

> "So then why, at times, do I feel that I should just be alone? Let me clarify this. Maybe every six months or so, I wonder if I am just not meant to be in a relationship. I have always been kind of a free spirit, independent, spur-of-the-moment kind of woman…These feelings, I have noticed, tend to come up when I am driving up the coast alone with the top down."

I was one of the guests on the NPR show about the reader and her question, and I wondered whether she might be single at heart. What I want to write about here is something else: the experience she describes as best capturing the allure of single life – "driving up the coast alone with the top down."

I thought about that when I read this paragraph from Kate Bolick's cover story in the ATLANTIC magazine, "All the single ladies":

> "Back when I believed my mother had a happy marriage…she surprised me by confiding that one of the most blissful

moments of her life had been when she was 21, driving down the highway in her VW Beetle, with nowhere to go except wherever she wanted to be. 'I had my own car, my own job, all the clothes I wanted,' she remembered wistfully. Why couldn't she have had more of that?"

Two single people from two different generations alighted on the same image of the joy of single life. The image captures freedom, and the idea of going places – those places being whatever you want them to be. An awesome car is part of it – either a convertible or a snug bug. There's also sunshine and a great view.

In years of doing scientific research on perceptions of single people, I've found that most beliefs are negative stereotypes. There is one exception: In just about every study, people say that they see single people as more independent than married or coupled people. The person driving along the coast with the top down does seem to be the picture of independence.

As a single-at-heart person with a sunroof-topped car, living along the California coast, I can relate. Yet the image captures only a sliver of the allure of single life. The person in the car is driving alone, but research shows that most single people are even more connected to siblings, parents, friends, and neighbors than married people are. What's more, when an ailing parent needs care, it is often the single sons or daughters, rather than the married ones, who take on more than their share of the responsibility.

For me, among the aspects of single life I find most attractive is the opportunity to create the balance between time-to-myself and time-with-others that is optimal for me. I savor my solitude, and I also love the time I spend with the people I care about the most.

The image of driving along the coast evokes an expansive sense of single life. That can be spectacular. So can a focused intensity. There are times, for example, when I am so into my writing that I just don't want to think about anything else or do anything else. I might ignore the phone or work way past the time when I would typically go to sleep. I love it that I live alone and can inhabit my writing "zone" (or whatever else has sucked me in) for as long as I like.

17.

Unfathomable Even to Brilliant, Kind, and Open Minds: The Securely Single

Secure in our single status, on Valentine's Day and every other day

February 8, 2010 by Bella DePaulo, Ph.D. at Psychology Today

Today, PSYCHOLOGY TODAY highlighted a quote from a blogger's recent post, "To be or not to be (in love): That is the question." The quote, referring to Valentine's Day and all the "survival guides" published to mark the day, was this: "Do we really get that close to death if we spend this day alone?" That made me think that the post would be an enlightened one, free of singlism and good for consciousness-raising about the full and meaningful lives of so many people who are living single.

My sense is that the blogger thinks she is trying to be fair to single people. For example, she says, "if you want to embrace your singleness, I just happened to jot down a few perks right here." But then look at those perks. They start with the fact that you are less likely to get a sexually transmitted disease and end with the supposedly reassuring message that you really can have someone after all because there are 904 dating services. Those are tips for EMBRACING my singleness?

Worse, though, are some of the other condescending, caricaturing, insulting claims she makes about people who are single. Here are some examples, all word-for-word from her post:

The blogger's 1, 2, 3

1. "Despite the plethora of books out there that declare people to OWN their single status, let's face it, most people aren't completely satisfied with their vibrators or Youporn."

2. "This scarlet lettering has inspired restaurants to hold anti-Valentine's Day themed dinners for bitter women."

3. Here's her #2 "perk" of single life: "NONE OF YOUR FRIENDS WILL RESENT YOU. For those of you in loving, committed

relationships that resemble picture frame stock photos, single people hate you, sorry."

These are the words of someone who believes herself to be open-minded but simply cannot fathom the possibility that single people can be secure in their single status. I'll try to offer some beginnings of an explanation here, but I hope the blogger will read some truly enlightened books about single life, such as Jaclyn Geller's Here Comes the Bride, Kay Trimberger's The New Single Woman, and my Singled Out and Single with Attitude.

Bella's corresponding 1, 2, 3

1. I love my single life. I pursue my passions and create the life that is most meaningful to me. I have the balance of sociability and solitude that is right for me. I have "The Ones" rather than "The One" - people in my life who care for me and I for them. Nasty quips about vibrators and Youporn do not speak to what I love about my single life.

2. The "bitter" stereotype is based in the presumption that all singles wish they were coupled. Not so. In a Pew survey (Pew is a research organization, not an advocacy group), the biggest proportion of single people, 55%, said they were not in a committed relationship AND that they were not looking for a partner. (Described more fully on p. 84 of Singled Out.) When you are happily and securely single, you can have dinner on Valentine's Day or any other day without even a wisp of bitterness.

3. I have friends and family who are in loving, committed relationships, including some who are married. I love them. I'm happy for them. The thing is, they are also happy for me. If you are secure in your own status, whether it is single or coupled, then you don't feel hatred toward people who do not share your status or your life choices. What is unfortunate is not the person whose life preferences and choices are different from your own, but the person who has prejudged you as a fragile, bitter, resentful, vibrator-clutching, porn-watching victim because of the life that you lead.

18.

Owning Our Good Feelings about Single Life

If you are happily single, don't get bullied into denying it

July 18, 2013 by Bella DePaulo, Ph.D in PsychCentral

The name of this blog, "Single at Heart," is telling. It describes people like me – at heart, we are single. It is how we live our most authentic and meaningful lives. We are not single because we have issues, or because we gave up on dating and decided to "settle" for being single. Living single is how we live our *best* lives. For many, such as myself, marriage would be a step down. It would be a bad fit with who we really are.

Of course, this is not the party line or the conventional wisdom. I have been studying single life for quite some time, so I am accustomed to the incredulous responses of people who cannot believe that anyone could *choose* to be single, or could be single and truly happy. Those sorts of people like to believe that we happy singles are just fooling ourselves.

Sometimes it is more than that. Research has shown that sometimes other people are actually mad at us for choosing to be single!

In an email exchange with a man I do not know, I answered one of his questions by explaining that I mostly write for and about single people who love living single. I do not write about dating or other ways to become unsingle.

He was having none of it. He claimed that single women do not want to be single and they do not enjoy single life. Specifically, he had this to say about you, my readers:

> *"[They] just get to a point in their lives where they say, 'I'm better off living my life on my terms because it is too short to put up with nonsense.'*

> *"And the other half lack ability to date desirable men."*

Then he added, *"That's different than wanting to be single. That is utilitarian, not preferable."*

He does not know any of you and he does not know me. But in his mind, he "knows" that we don't really want to be single. Instead, he thinks we are single either because we got totally frustrated with dating or because we "lack ability." I don't doubt that some single people fit his descriptions but he seems to doubt that *any* single people fit my description of what it means to be single at heart.

I don't think he has any bad intentions, and I know he has lots of company in thinking the way he does. In fact, it is because these kinds of mistaken beliefs about single people are so widespread that I wanted to address them here.

The type of argument being advanced here is significant. He is *not* saying: studies show that single people are unhappy, and if only they would marry, that would change. I have debunked that claim many times before.

Instead, he seems to be saying that he does not believe what you say about your own feelings. If you say you enjoy your single life, his response is that you don't really feel that way – you are just saying that you do because you have decided to settle or you "lack ability to date desirable men." It is an argument based on presumptuousness – the type of argument I have heard and discussed before.

It is a difficult argument to counter because whatever you say in response can and probably will be discounted. It is an argument that denies you ownership of your own feelings or any insight into them. People who make these arguments think they know you better than you do, even though they have never met you.

I hope you will not be worn down by such arguments. More than 3,500 people have taken the survey, "Are you single at heart?" I doubt that the thousands of people who recorded single-at-heart type answers are all just fooling themselves.

19.

A Singles Manifesto, from a Pioneer

Singles Manifesto: Will it stick this time?

March 3, 2009 by Bella DePaulo, Ph.D. at Psychology Today

Optimistically, I like to think that the writing and research and public speaking that I do about living single is in the service of social change. I like to smash myths (especially the ones that purport to have scientific backing, only they don't), underscore inequities, and point to the strengths that so many singles demonstrate despite all the relentless singlism and matrimania that permeates society. You might even say that I'd like to start a revolution, or at least a singles movement.

So I was more than a little surprised when I discovered that there already was such a movement, not so very long ago. I learned this from a headline in the LOS ANGELES TIMES last week: "Marie Barbare Edwards dies at 89; psychologist helped pioneer a 'singles pride' movement."

Edwards had written a book, The Challenge of Being Single, in 1974. The same year, the LOS ANGELES TIMES wrote about her in an article titled, "A Singles' Lib Manifesto."

Of course, I immediately searched for the book. Holding it in my hands, I was both delighted at what I found and sorry that I had not known about it when I wrote Singled Out. Edwards did not write a social-science based book in the way that I did (though with her degrees from Stanford and UCLA, she could have); still, in spirit, I now consider her my intellectual godmother.

Consider just a few highlights from THE CHALLENGE OF BEING SINGLE:

In the first chapter, she begins by gently mocking the question, "How come you're not married?" It is, she quips, the equivalent of being challenged to "prove that you're not a freak."

Among the errors and **myths** she describes are:

- Finding the one-and-only will solve all of your problems.

- All single women want to get married.

- All single men are afraid of responsibility.

- All unmarrieds are terribly lonely.

- Single life is hazardous because there will be no one around to help you if you are hurt or sick.

What, according to Edwards (and her co-author, Eleanor Hoover), is the end result of all of these stereotypes and myths? Discrimination. Again getting there before I did, she spells out the unfair costs to being single in taxes, the workplace, insurance, and housing. She does not see singles simply as victims, though, and ends with a chapter on the greatest advantage of being single and with her manifesto.

SINGLES MANIFESTO

Edwards' book includes the complete Singles Manifesto, consisting of a Preamble, three Articles (attitudes toward self, others, and society), and 17 statements. Here, for your reading pleasure, are some excerpts from this 1974 proclamation.

PREAMBLE of Marie Edwards' SINGLES MANIFESTO:

Whereas the written and spoken word about singles has been and continues to be one of gloom and doom, untruths and misinformation, we the singles of the United States - divorced, separated, and never-married - in order to bury the myths, establish the truths, uplift our spirits, promote our freedom, become cognizant of our great fortune as singles, do ordain and establish this manifesto for the singles of the United States of America.

SAMPLE STATEMENTS from Marie Edwards' 1974 SINGLES MANIFESTO:

• I will, in my deepest feelings, know that it's okay to be single and, becoming braver, know that it's even more than okay - it can be a great and untapped opportunity for continuous personal growth.

• I will stop searching for the "one-and-only," knowing that as I become more free to be myself, I will be freer to care about others, so that relationships will come to me as a natural consequence and I will feel free to accept or reject them.

• Instead of searching for the "one-and-only," I will realize the tremendous importance of friendships.

• I will no longer suffer in silence the injustices to me as a single, but will do everything I can to eradicate them.

• I will, by choosing to live a free single life, be helping to raise the status of singlehood. In doing this, I will be strengthening rather than weakening marriage, for when we truly have the option not to marry, marriage will be seen as a free choice rather than one demanded by a pairing society.

When Will Singles Awareness "Stick"?

Discovering Marie Edwards, the singles pioneer from decades past, reminded me of the experience I had while gathering materials for the first course I taught on singles in society. I found a number of academic articles, published years or even decades earlier, that all started or ended with the lament that there is just too little scholarly attention paid to people who are single. As I continued to prepare my course, I realized that the state of the scholarship had not changed much - there was still far too little serious research and thinking about the place of singles in society.

There are similar trends in the popular press. Edwards' Singles Manifesto is again a relevant example; it was published in the LOS ANGELES TIMES in 1974, but it did not stick.

There are no long-enduring singles advocacy groups, comparable, say, to AARP. The American Association for Single People (AASP) did some important work for a while, then got tripped up by financial challenges, and is now an informational resource. Its advocacy work is now pursued by the Alternatives to Marriage Project (AtMP).

The question now is, Will any of this stick? Will scholarship on singles gain momentum? Will the number of singles-relevant courses increase and earn a permanent place in the college curriculum? Will advocacy groups strengthen and multiply? Will awareness of singlism and matrimania take permanent hold in our society?

III.

Mocking Those 'Why Are You Single' Lists

20.

The Last 'Why You Are Single' List You Will Ever Need

Block that click! No more singles-bashing lists

June 11, 2012 by Bella DePaulo, Ph.D. at Psychology Today

I'm not biting. I'm not reading, I'm not clicking. Bloggers and single-shamers can post as many derogatory 'why you aren't married yet' posts as they'd like, but I'm not mentioning them and I'm not linking to them.

That was the post I started to write.

Then Nicole sent me a link to a post by Samhita Mukhopadhyay over at JEZEBEL. (Thanks, Nicole!) The title is "Ten very good reasons you aren't married yet." Nicole is someone whose opinions I trust. She said she liked everything about the post except the word "yet" in the title, so I went ahead and read it.

Mukhopadhyay begins by taking on Tracy McMillan, who is continuing her bashing of single women with a book and still another blog post telling them what they did wrong and thereby landed in perpetual singledom. There is so much wrong with that attitude, and readers of my books and blogs already know all about that.

As Mukhopadhyay notes, few of McMillan's writings (or other similar ones)

> "offer solace; instead, the reader gets shaming advice and tough love about how she is a crazed angry, clingy (or too independent, get your story straight), desperate b*tch who has to try harder." [NOTE: The word was spelled out at Jezebel. Not sure we can do that here at PT.]

I find the mere question, "So why have you never been married?," offensive and inappropriate, regardless of whether it is aimed at single women or single men or both, and I have mocked it in previous posts. In this one, I began by noting:

Questions like that push my perversity button, and I can't help generating Q & A sequences. For example:

CLUELESS QUESTION: "So why have you never been married?"
MY PERVERSE ANSWER: So why have you never been an accountant?

CLUELESS QUESTION: "Why aren't you married?"
MY PERVERSE ANSWER: Why aren't you a Christmas tree?

CLUELESS QUESTION: "When are you going to get married?"
MY PERVERSE ANSWER: When did you last have sex?

CLUELESS QUESTION: "Will you ever marry?"
MY PERVERSE ANSWER: Maybe if I get hit on the head with a rock and turn into a different person.

If you want my serious answer to the question of why I, personally, am single, it is simple: I am single at heart. Single is who I really am. Single life is the most authentic and meaningful life for me.

In Mukhopadhyay's list of reasons, the one that comes closest to the single-at-heart answer is this:

You legitimately just don't want to get married.

"No, you are not lying to yourself; you actually just don't want to get married. You've been to lots of weddings, you appreciated some of the sentiments, you were happy for everyone, but you didn't walk out wishing it were you that got married."

Mukhopadhyay recognizes that not everyone is single-at-heart. Importantly, she also realizes that even if you want to be married eventually – maybe even if you wish you were already married – the fact that you are single does not mean that you and all of the other single women are "crazy, angry, slutty liars."

Here are a few more of the reasons from her list:

You are focused on your career.

"And you are not going to apologize for it. Some people call this being a 'b*tch,' because you are a lady and you have a job that you might be more focused on than smiling pretty and making sure you don't intimidate Mr. Right. Most of us just call this being alive in 2012 (you know the time the economy tanked and we had to work to eat)."

You can't afford it.

"…men don't feel ready to propose until they have the cash to support a family. There is no special Spanx you can buy that will bolster a man's self-esteem to convince him that you don't care he is broke."

You've got a life and friends that you are happy with.

"If a dude shows up that's cool, but you are not sweating it because every day is an awesome new adventure full of phone calls from loved ones, cupcakes, yoga classes and dance parties. You enjoy each minute, focus on the positive and when you are down (a symptom of life, not just single life) you have 500 friends to call, because you have spent time on all types of relationships, not just the kind that will lead to marriage. Friendship-the realest investment a lady can make."

21.

'Why Are You Single?' Meets 'Why Are You Married?'

The question married people are never asked

February 19, 2011 by Bella DePaulo, Ph.D. at Psychology Today

Yeah, I've seen it. The picture of the oh-so-sad single woman splayed across Yahoo, next to the story titled, "Why are you single?" This story line is, of course, utterly predictable. People who are single have some explaining to do. In this particular iteration, the condescending author tells singles that they are not even getting their explanations right. She pats them on the head and tell them to perk up - then their dreamboat will come.

Do you think I'm already exaggerating? Then go straight to the author's bottom line. After schooling singles on their overly pessimistic ways of thinking, she ends on this note about how to find a relationship (and of course, to her, 'relationship' has only one narrow meaning):

> "...decide right now that you're meant to be in one and watch the dating world flock to you and your aura of optimism."

The opening line is just as bad:

> "If you're single, I'm sure you've asked yourself more than once: 'WHY ME?'"

No, I haven't.

Stories like this always tempt me to rewrite the examples of faulty thinking that singles engage in as examples of faulty thinking that married people engage in. A funny thing happened this time, though: I found that the 'lessons' needed hardly any repackaging.

Take, for example, this line of thinking that the author ascribes to single people. She believes (not on the basis of any evidence, as far as I can tell) that what single people offer as an explanation for why they are not married is:

> "I'm not attractive/smart/rich/young/hot enough."

See how easy this is? With no evidence needed, I can just make stuff up. So, what might a married person offer as an explanation as to why they are not single?

"I'm not attractive/smart/rich/young/hot enough."

Or how about this one? The author thinks that singles also use another explanation as to why they are single:

"I'm BETTER at being single. I guess I'm just supposed to stay single forever."

Here, we can turn this into a married person's explanation for why they are married by searching for and replacing just one word:

"I'm BETTER at being married. I guess I'm just supposed to stay married forever."

The other examples work, too. From the article about faulty explanations for staying single:

"I'm cursed. I'll never meet anyone."

My parallel explanation for staying married:

"I'm cursed. I'll never meet anyone."

While the author was making up explanations that singles offer for why they are single, she missed out on the one documented repeatedly by actual data:

I'm single because I want to be. I CHOSE this life.

The whole story was based on the premise that no one would actually want to be single. You never see stories about the kinds of married-person explanations I posited in my parody because married people are not asked to defend their marital status. They have no explaining to do.

22.

About Those 27 Wrong Reasons You Are Single

There are so many right reasons to be single

February 20, 2014 by Bella DePaulo, Ph.D. at Psychology Today

When I'm ambivalent about addressing a particular topic, sometimes hearing from readers tips the balance. That just happened with Sara Eckel's new book, *It's not you: 27 (wrong) reasons you're single*, and the press about it. Enough people have asked me what I think that I just had to take a look.

I was reluctant because I have an aversion to the "why are you single" genre and that tainted my expectations, even knowing that Eckel was out to debunk all those patronizing, contradictory, and inaccurate nuggets of advice that are offered to single people, supposedly to help them become unsingle. Also, having written an article called, "The last 'why are you single' list you will ever need"—plus an array of posts on related themes (see below)—it did seem to be time to move on.

On the other hand, I knew she was a good writer from some of her previous work. Plus, she checked with me before the book went to print on what she wanted to say about my writings on single life. That meant two more points in her favor—she was including my point of view, and she cared about accuracy.

Sara Eckel is writing from a very different perspective than my own— she got married at 39, and really wanted to be married much sooner. I never want to get married and never did want to marry. So reading about her experiences and those of her single friends, some of whom also stayed single well into their 30s (or are still single but do not want to be), was a bit like delving into anthropology. Oh, so that's what it's like?

I think I've missed out on a lot of pain. Again and again, Eckel talks about how lonely and distressing it was to spend still another Saturday evening home alone watching TV. Each time, I thought about how much I enjoy spending Saturday evenings home alone watching Netflix. Not that I'd want to spend every night like that—I enjoy my time out with friends (and family when we're on the same coast), or home watching Netflix with them, and I like to do other things, too. But I never once have felt badly because it was Saturday night and I did not have a romantic partner.

Now I HAVE felt badly about being excluded from social events when many of my friends were coupled and they socialized mostly only with other couples. I objected to needing a romantic partner to be included, not to not having such a partner.

Sara Eckel is an engaging writer who lets her vulnerabilities show. I have been reading her book and her other related writings with more interest than I had anticipated. The best thing about her writings, for me, is that she never forgets that not everyone wants to be coupled, and that plenty of single people are living the life that is right for them.

Here are a few examples. First, from an essay in Salon:

> "…women are delaying and forgoing marriage **because they can**." [Note how she includes not just women who are delaying marriage but also those who are forgoing it.]

> "…what is perhaps most impressive about single women today is their ability to build rich, meaningful lives without any sort of blueprint. It takes courage to stay true to yourself when so many voices are telling you to follow a more conventional path."

Now, here are just a few of the many examples from *It's Not You*:

> "As I speak with other people who stayed single well into their adulthood—and whose unattached state was not a choice…." [notice the important qualifier]

> "When you are a single person who would rather not be…" [again, notice that she makes it clear that she is not talking about all single people]

> [Here, she makes that point explicitly:] "I don't presume to speak for all singles. Of course, many people are happily unattached or are searching but don't trouble themselves with the question, 'What's wrong?'"

> [Also here:] "…I certainly know that there are plenty of people who genuinely adore their solo life—the freedom, the travel, the deep peace that comes from living in a home where everything is arranged exactly as you like it."

I don't love the use of the term "unattached" to refer to single people, since most single people do have genuine attachment relationships—they just aren't attached to a spouse. But I think she does recognize that point, as when she notes that a sense of intimacy, closeness, and connection "doesn't necessarily have to come from a romantic partnership."

I've been talking mostly about the tone of the book, but I also appreciated the substance. Consider, for example, her analysis of the double standard with regard to credit for the tasks you do as a single person versus a married one. As a married person, she notes, her husband does some of the things she had to cover when she was single. Yet, you can "still get full credit for being an adult—MORE credit than if you were handling everything on your own…In many ways, I was never more adult than when I was single."

In a way, what Eckel is trying to do in *Its Not You* is the same thing I set out to do in *Singled Out* (and in my blogs and other writings)—bust myths about single people. Eckel, though, draws mostly from her own experiences and those of her friends, whereas I rely more heavily on scientific data. I think the two approaches can complement each other.

23.

Why Are You Single? International Edition

Here's what single people say about their single lives

September 2, 2014 by Bella DePaulo, Ph.D at PsychCentral

By now, you have probably seen far too many of those "why are you single" articles. Way too often, the authors treat singlehood as a disease that needs to be cured, and they tell you what you did wrong that led you to get (or stay) sick. I've made fun of those singles-bashing lists and also offered some more positive takes on single life in The Real Reasons for Living Single.

In addition to the disease-mentality, there is something else that is troubling about those articles – they are almost always just the opinions of some outside observer. They rarely ask single people what they think about their single lives.

Happily, that has changed with a new typology offered by the Polish sociologist Julita Czernecka, author of *Single and the City*. She asked a select group of Polish single people – 30 men and 30 women – to talk about their single lives. The people she interviewed are not a representative sample of Polish singles, so her results are more suggestive than definitive. I think they provide a good alternative, though, to people who offer nothing but their own opinion as to why other people are single.

The 60 singles Czernecka interviewed fit the profile of people she was most interested in learning about. They were financially stable college graduates between the ages of 27 and 41 who had not been in a serious romantic relationship for at least two years. None had ever been married and none had children, but they were all still old enough to have children if they ever wanted to.

Here are the 5 types of single people she found. (She did not say how many were in each category.)

1. **Happy singles**: These are single people who "fully accept their lifestyle." They "do not feel the need to be in a relationship." In fact, they say that they are happy not to be in a serious romantic relationship. They are probably the people I would call *single at heart*.

2. **Accustomed singles**: They are similar in many ways to the happy singles, but instead of saying that they are happy with their single lives, they say, "I'm used to being single." They don't mean that in any resigned or negative sense. As Czernecka explains, "They have been alone for a while and treat it as their natural state – they do not want to destroy the harmony of their life, or give up their rituals and everyday pleasures for a partner. All emotional needs, the sense of being accepted and of help in everyday life are provided by their family and friends, which is why they say that they 'do not need anyone else.'"

3. **Hurt singles**: They have had bad experiences with romantic relationships in the past and do not want to be hurt again. (The Carly Simon lyrics, "haven't got time for the pain," sound relevant here.)

4. **All-or-nothing singles**: They only want to be with a romantic partner if they can find someone great. They are not going to be in a romantic relationship just to be in a romantic relationship.

5. **Romantics**: These people are a lot like the all-or-nothings, only with a much more romantic bent. They seem to believe in the fairy tales and the myths. They are sure that their "soul mate" is out there somewhere. Some have broken off decent relationships because their partner did not make them swoon the way they expect to when they finally find their true Princess or Prince Charming.

It is an interesting typology because it acknowledges the many ways that single people think about their single lives. The author does not just assume that all single people want to become unsingle and are trying to figure out what problems they have that might need to be fixed. It would be useful to see this typology tested with bigger and more representative samples.

IV.

The Good Life and the Successful Life

24.

Elements of a Good Life: Our List Is Way Too Short

Missing passions, people, and meanings

April 22, 2013 by Bella DePaulo, Ph.D at PsychCentral

Anyone can offer advice for living the good life – no qualifications are necessary – and many people do. Those who have gotten the most attention lately include Sheryl Sandburg with her book, *Lean In*, the haughty Princeton mother telling the undergraduate women at her alma mater to grab a Princeton man while the grabbing is good, Ann Marie Slaughter telling women they actually can't have it all, and now Elsa Walsh in the *Washington Post*, telling women to settle for a good-enough life.

What is striking about all of these offerings is just how stunningly limited the components of a good life seem to be, in the eyes of these self-appointed sages. The conversation is all about three domains: work, marriage, and children.

For those of us who are single-at-heart, there is potentially so much more. I think that even for people who care most about the tired three, there is more about life that attracts their interest and maybe even their passion.

First, consider the people part of the equation. A spouse and offspring are fine for those who want them, but what about all of the other people who matter? What about friends and siblings and cousins and nieces and nephews and aunts and uncles and grandparents? What about mentors and teachers and other special people who helped us and believed in us all along the way? What about colleagues and neighbors and fellow members of groups that welcome us, be they political or religious or civic or educational or athletic or artistic?

How about the draw of time away from people? We who are single-at-heart cherish our solitude. It refreshes us, offers us space to be creative or contemplative or to pursue what interests us, on our own terms and in our own time.

How can we talk about work without recognizing its many forms, from the onerous to the exhilarating? There's the work we do to pay the bills and the work we might do even if we were not paid for it.

Where, in the tripartite equation, is a place for contributing to a cause that reaches beyond your own nuclear family? Where does volunteering fit in, or spirituality, or pursuing social justice, or creating works of art or encouraging thoughtfulness or working toward a more sustainable planet? What about those who want to lead a more expansive life? Or those who like to focus intently on one particular passion? How about those who want to live a simple life – why isn't that a valued choice?

I'm sure there is much more that could be added to my list. I'd like to hear about what I missed. Mostly, I'd love to see our high-profile conversations steer themselves out of the marriage-kids-work rut and soar into more imaginative spaces.

25.

Singles Value Meaningful Work
– And Did So Even in High School

Singles are more intrinsically motivated at work

November 30, 2010 by Bella DePaulo, Ph.D. at Psychology Today

Meaningful work should be one of life's prizes. Imagine working not (just) because you need the money but because you are passionate about what you do. You find your work interesting, challenging; you like that you get to use your skills, solve problems, learn things, and maybe even help other people.

If you are married and you feel that way about your work, you are probably admired for it. If you are single, there is some risk that you will instead be pitied. The attitude sometimes is (toward women, especially) that you don't "really" love what you do - you are just telling yourself that. Or you are compensating for not having what is truly important in life - a spouse.

What if we could assess people's attitudes toward work before marrying becomes much of an issue - for example, when they are adolescents, still in high school? It has been done.

In 1991, 709 Minnesota high school seniors (none married, none who were parents) were asked what would be important to them when looking for work. The two main categories that were assessed were intrinsic rewards and extrinsic ones. The extrinsically motivated adolescents cared mostly about how much they would get paid, whether the work would be steady, and whether there would be opportunities for advancement. Intrinsically motivated adolescents wanted the work to be meaningful - challenging, interesting, and full of opportunities to learn, to use skills, be responsible, and solve problems.

Nine years later, when those participants were 26 or 27 years old, the adolescents who had said they were looking for secure jobs with good pay were more likely to be married (and to be parents). Those who were more interested in meaningful work were more likely to be single (and they were less likely to have kids).

At ages 26 or 27, the participants were asked once again to indicate what was important to them about their work. Those who were married valued meaningful work less than single men and women did. So the study documented two consistent links between intrinsic motivation and marital status. Those who valued meaningful work when they were in high school were more likely to be single 9 years later. Even taking that into account, those who married were less likely to value meaningful work when they were 26 or 27 years old than those who were single.

The implications of being a parent by age 26 or 27 were more complex. For example, married mothers cared less about extrinsic motivations such as pay, whereas single mothers cared more. Fathers cared more about meaningful work only if they were cohabiting (and not married). As is typical for good research, other factors (such as level of education, current employment status, and income level) were ruled out as explanations of the results.

I'll add my usual disclaimer that social science studies tell us about trends, and not about what happens in every individual life. There are always plenty of exceptions. Also, the study I'm discussing does not say that you need to choose between meaningful work and marriage. Instead, I think it suggests that many singles who say that they care about the quality of their work experiences really mean it. They always have, at least as far back as high school.

26.

Success Depends More on Friendship Skills than Romantic Ones

Having a romantic partner matters less than you think

August 30, 2013 by Bella DePaulo, Ph.D. at Psychology Today

If you are around the age of 20, you probably have something on your mind – or maybe just lodged in the back of your mind. In our matrimaniacal culture, obsessed as it is with marriage and coupling and romantic "achievements," you probably can't help but wonder about your own romantic skills.

Once we get past all this over-the-top hyping of coupling, and realize that there are people of every age who are perfectly happy living single (and some, such as the single-at-heart, who live their best lives single), then we will all be better able to live the lives best suited to each of us as individuals.

In the meantime, it is great when there is some myth-shattering research that challenges our cultural fantasies about the overriding importance of being good at romance.

Here's the question the study addressed: Suppose we measure how talented and successful 20-somethings are at friendship and at romance; to what extent would those age-20 talents predict success 10 years later in their work life, as well as in their friendships and romance? So, if you are good at friendship at age 20, are you likely to be doing better in your work life at age 30 than if you were not good at friendship as a 20-year old? What about your romantic talents at age 20 – how relevant are they to your success at age 30?

Researchers have been studying 205 Minnesotans since they were between the ages of 8 and 12 years old. Around age 20 and then 10 years later, they assessed how skilled and successful the participants were at friendships and romantic relationships. At age 30, the researchers also assessed success at work: "a clear track record of reliably holding and successfully executing the responsibilities of paid positions."

To measure friendship skills and romantic talents, the researchers used the participants' own reports (from several sources, such as validated self-report measures and, at age 20, in-person interviews), reports from their parents, and the evaluations of clinical psychologists who saw the participants' self-reported data. For friendship, the assessments were designed primarily to assess whether the participant had "a close, confiding friendship," though other indications of having a social life were included, too. For romance, the key question was whether the participant "had engaged in a close and positive reciprocal relationship with a romantic partner for more than a brief period." The 30-year olds were asked whether they had such relationships within the past 3 years.

The results?

Friendship skills at age 20 matter for success at age 30. People who were good at friendship at age 20 were more likely to be succeeding at paid work 10 years later than those who were not good at friendship. Unsurprisingly, those who were especially good at friendship at age 20 were also especially good at friendship at age 30. And guess what? They were also good at romance.

Romantic skill at age 20 did not predict any successes at age 30, not even romantic ones! The 20-somethings who had had "a close and positive reciprocal relationship with a romantic partner for more than a brief period" were no more likely to be successful at work 10 years later than those who did not have such a partner. They were also no more likely to be successful at friendships. And, those who had a good and lasting romantic relationship at age 20 were no more (or less) likely to have such a relationship 10 years later!

So if you are a 20-year old and you think you are good at romance, good for you. Enjoy it for its own sake. But if you are a 20-year old and you are good at friendship, you have something to be truly proud of – something that will last and which may even predict success in the future.

Reference:

Roisman, G. I., Masten, A. S., Coatsworth, J. D., & Tellegen, A. (2004). Salient and emerging developmental tasks in the transition to adulthood. *Child Development*, 75, 123-133.

27.

What Counts as "Having It All" for You?

More imaginative meanings of "having it all"

January 23, 2012 by Bella DePaulo, Ph.D at PsychCentral

To a dramatically greater extent than decades ago, you get to create your own life path. Gone are the days when the standard path through adult life was to get married very young, have kids, stayed married, and have grandkids. Gone, too, are the days when people often stayed with the same company for a lifetime.

Now we can stay single or cohabit or get married or cycle through different relationship statuses over the course of our lives. We can choose to have kids or to not have kids. We can try new jobs (though sometimes by necessity rather than choice). We can pursue an education, then do something else, then go back to school again.

Or we can go straight into the workforce, skipping any higher education. (Statistically, our opportunities are more limited if that's what we choose, but there are some who succeed spectacularly well without a college degree.)

My mother had six siblings and my father had one. Growing up, all of them lived in or very close to the same town. One of my aunts had grown children who lived in a home right behind hers. Families can still live that way, but it is no longer all that unusual to find family members scattered from coast to coast and everywhere in between.

With so many options for designing our own lives, it is puzzling that concepts such as "having it all" have such limited meanings. About a decade ago, I made a huge change in my life, and realized that what "having it all" meant to me was strikingly different than the usual understanding. I wrote about that in the opening to Chapter 10 of Singled Out.

EXCERPT from *Singled Out*, **p. 185**:

After I moved from the East Coast to the West, there was a time when I knew I wanted to stay out West, but was not yet sure whether I could make that happen. Would I be able to sell my home in Virginia? Would anyone hire me for only as many hours as it took to pay my bills, so I could devote the rest of my time, and all of my heart and soul, to the study of singles? What about all the rest of it – would it all work out? Then one day, I got a phone call, and I knew that it had happened. I hung up and sat in quiet stunned amazement for a moment. Then I thought to myself, "I can have it all."

It took a second for me to realize just how bizarre that thought was – at least by the prevailing standards. Here I was, stepping into a life in which I had no husband, no children, no full-time job, and for the first time in more than a decade, no home that I owned. Yet to me, I was about to have it all.

I doubt that I would have thought of my life that way many years before. I loved my friends, my family, my job, and my home, but I would not have spontaneously appropriated a cultural catch-phrase, nor refashioned it so thoroughly.

V.

Savoring Our Solitude:
Choosing to Spend Time Alone

28.

The American Psyche: Tipping Toward Solitude?

I'm never bored when I'm alone

August 21, 2008 by Bella DePaulo, Ph.D. at Psychology Today

I live in the most ordinary American household - I live alone. Knock on any door in the nation and you are more likely to find a household like mine than a household with mom, dad, and the kids, or a household with a married couple and no kids, or a single-parent household, or any other kind.

There has been a surge in the number of single-person households, and a decline in the number of married-with-kids households. This is not a fad - it is a decades-long demographic juggernaut. It has many pundits and prognosticators plenty worried.

One of their fears is that we may be on the cusp of an epidemic of loneliness. Interventions, they say, may be in order. Some even present statistics in support of the link between living alone and feeling lonely. Not bogus statistics but real ones. For example, a recent report about the well-being of older people in the UK noted that 17% of older people living alone say that they are often lonely, compared to only 2% of those living with others.

That's a meaningful difference. I do believe that many older people are isolated, lonely, and depressed (though not as many as our stereotypes would lead us to believe). Their problems should be taken seriously. But let's not make a pathology out of a preference.

Think again about the statistic that 17% of older people living alone report that they often feel lonely. What strikes me about this finding is that 83% of older people living alone do NOT often feel lonely. Remember that they are old, some may have health problems that limit their mobility, others may have close friends and family who have died, and they are living without anyone under the same roof readily available for small talk or interesting excursions. Yet 83% say that they are not often lonely.

When I was writing Singled Out, I read voraciously about demographic patterns (such as the increase in 1-person households) and about loneliness, and thought a lot about my own life. I live alone and I am almost never lonely. I am also rarely bored. Then I realized something that seemed startling at first: During those atypical times when I am bored, I am almost always with other people. I'm never bored when I'm alone.

I don't consider myself an introvert. I love to socialize (with people who do not bore me), I love the visits (time-limited) from friends and family who come to catch up with me and soak up the sun from my deck, and I love to entertain. But I also cherish my solitude.

Introverts and loners: They are not apologizing anymore

Jonathan Rauch does consider himself an introvert. In 2003, he wrote an essay for the ATLANTIC magazine that began like this:

> DO YOU KNOW SOMEONE WHO NEEDS HOURS ALONE EVERY DAY? WHO LOVES QUIET CONVERSATIONS ABOUT FEELINGS OR IDEAS, AND CAN GIVE A DYNAMITE PRESENTATION TO A BIG AUDIENCE, BUT SEEMS AWKWARD IN GROUPS AND MALADROIT AT SMALL TALK? WHO HAS TO BE DRAGGED TO PARTIES AND THEN NEEDS THE REST OF THE DAY TO RECUPERATE? WHO GROWLS OR SCOWLS OR GRUNTS OR WINCES WHEN ACCOSTED WITH PLEASANTRIES BY PEOPLE WHO ARE JUST TRYING TO BE NICE?
>
> IF SO, DO YOU TELL THIS PERSON HE IS 'TOO SERIOUS,' OR ASK IF HE IS OKAY? REGARD HIM AS ALOOF, ARROGANT, RUDE? REDOUBLE YOUR EFFORTS TO DRAW HIM OUT?
>
> IF YOU ANSWERED YES TO THESE QUESTIONS, CHANCES ARE THAT YOU HAVE AN INTROVERT ON YOUR HANDS - AND THAT YOU AREN'T CARING FOR HIM PROPERLY.

Rauch, a prolific writer, got more enthusiastic responses to that essay than to anything else he had ever written. Three years later, the ATLANTIC reported that readers were still clicking their approval: Online, no other piece had drawn more traffic than Rauch's "Caring for Your Introvert."

The same year that Rauch's essay appeared, the witty and wonderful Party of One: The Loners' Manifesto was also published. Loners, notes author

Anneli Rufus, are people who prefer to be alone. They are not sad, lonely, or deranged.

Contrary to stereotypes and TV-punditry, loners are not serial murderers and they are not school shooters, either. True, there are criminals who look like loners, in that they spend lots of time alone. Typically, though, they are just pseudo-loners, who never craved all that time to themselves. They wanted to be included but were instead rejected.

True loners do not withdraw in order to stew in misery or plot violent revenge. Instead, Rufus reminds us, loners "know better than anyone how to entertain themselves...They have a knack for imagination, concentration, inner discipline, and invention."

Not all introverts or loners live alone. Their experiences, though, should give pause to those whose thoughts leap to loneliness when imagining the experiences of solo-dwellers, and to those who are tempted to swoop in with their interventions to rescue people who may be perfectly content exactly as they are.

Togetherness can also breed loneliness

The same report that underscored a link between living alone and feeling lonely also implicated divorce in the mix. As one headline put it, "Easy divorce has left elderly lonely and depressed."

The logic is that people who are divorced, and who also feel lonely, are lonely because they are divorced. Probably a good number really are.

The reverse sequence, though, should not be discounted. Some people divorce because they are lonely in their marriages. In the anthology, Women on Divorce, several contributors described such experiences. Ann Hood, for example, said, "I wanted my old pre-marriage back...I remembered how at night I used to sleep well. How being alone felt fine because there was no one down the hall not talking to me." Daphne Merkin added, "I, for instance, married a man who left me feeling lonely not because he wasn't home but because he was."

Preferences for togetherness can change over the course of your life

When I arrived at my first academic job at the age of 26, I considered it my great good fortune to have colleagues who wanted to go out to lunch every day. Now, 28 years later, if I had to go out to lunch every day - even with people I really like - I would go stark raving mad.

Early theorists of aging believed that with age came isolation. Some thought that older people were socially marginalized by a society preoccupied with youth. Others believed that older people wanted to withdraw from society, so they isolated themselves on purpose.

Then along came Laura Carstensen and her colleagues, who actually studied the social interaction preferences of people of different ages. Carstensen found that older people socialize more selectively. They still spend time with the people to whom they feel closest. They don't bother as much, though, with people they do not know so well, or with people who annoy them. That's by choice.

Tipping toward solitude

If there is such a thing as a national psyche, then I think the American version is showing signs of change. Think of trends such as the growing number of people who live alone, the growing preference for working from home, the increasing inclination for families (who have the means to do so) to give their kids rooms of their own, and the preference for older people to live independently as long as possible (instead of moving in with other family members, as they once did). There are many possible reasons for each of these trends, but perhaps at least some of the people in each of the categories have one thing in common: They like their time alone.

In all of our lives, we negotiate a balance between the time we spend with others and the time we spend alone. There are, and always will be, big individual differences. Some love the constant give-and-take of the company of other people, and others prefer more alone time.

Of course, humans are social beings. Meaningful relationships with other people, and time spent with others, will always be important. Still, if there were a national average of the solitude-sociability balance, and if that average were computed over time, I bet it would show that the American scales are tipping toward solitude.

29.

Sweet Solitude: Two Meanings of Alone

Time spent alone is not just about loneliness

March 20, 2011 by Bella DePaulo, Ph.D. at Psychology Today

"YOU POOR THING - YOU'RE 'ALONE' - YOU 'DON'T HAVE ANYONE." I've been railing against this use of the word ALONE to describe single people for a long, long time. To say that single people are ALONE, in this sense, is to believe that unless you have a spouse or romantic partner, you don't have anyone. By this manner of thinking, all of the other important people in our lives, such as friends, relatives, neighbors, mentors, and colleagues, just aren't anyone at all.

There is another meaning of ALONE, though, that also gets pinned on single people, and in a bad way. That's the time that we spend with no one else around. More than 31 million of us live alone. (That's a striking number, but because more than 100 million Americans are divorced, widowed, or have always been single, it falls far short of the majority of us.) Of course, even living alone does not preclude the possibility of having other people around - even lots of them - but it can add up to lots of time spent with no other hovering humans.

Those who would pity us for the time we spend ALONE think of our experiences as **LONELINESS**. That's the negative sense of being by yourself - having no other humans present with whom you can connect in a meaningful way, but wishing that you did. Surely, there are singles who feel lonely when they are in their homes (or even out and about) on their own, just as there are coupled people who feel lonely when their romantic partner is not at their side. But there is far more to the experience of being alone than feeling miserable and lonely. There is a reason (actually lots of them) why solitude is so often called sweet. We just don't hear about that as often.

Researchers in psychology need to own up to their fare share of the blame in this equation of spending time alone (or living alone) with loneliness. Type SOLITUDE into PsycInfo, probably the most comprehensive database for scholarly articles in psychology, and you will get 592 references. Doesn't sound so bad, until you take a close look at them and realize how few are based on empirical research (those articles are tagged as phenomenology, psychoanalysis, narratives, and spirituality, among other categories) and how many construe solitude in a bad way. (For example, #13 of the 592 is about "anxious solitude.") Now type in LONELINESS, and you get 5,128 references.

Slowly - very slowly - this is beginning to change. Christopher Long and James Averill wrote an article that provides the theoretical grounding that future empirical researchers can use as a guide. "Solitude: An exploration of the benefits of being alone," appeared in the JOURNAL FOR THE THEORY OF SOCIAL BEHAVIOR in 2003 (vol. 33, pp. 21-44). Now, when I check back to see if anything new on solitude has popped up in PsycInfo, I am sometimes pleasantly surprised.

Notwithstanding all of the psychologists fretting about loneliness, real people living their real lives often seem to crave time alone, then savor it when they get it. That's my sense, based mostly on unsystematic observations. (For example: A 2008 post, The American psyche: Tipping toward solitude?, has been one of my most popular. A more recent one, Extraversion and the single person, has also been popular.) It is time for researchers to show us the numbers.

It is not only when you are home alone that you can experience solitude. Solitude also happens in nature and even when you are alone in a crowd. I'm withholding Long and Averill's definition of solitude for now, because it would give away too much of what I'd like you to think about while I work on the second part in this series. If you like this topic, generate your own ideas of what's so sweet about solitude. (Post them in the comments section if you are willing.) Think not just about emotional aspects (though those surely matter a lot), but also cognitive and intellectual ones. (For example, are you smarter or more creative when you are on your own?) Consider, too, the big questions of who you are and who you want to be, what (and whom) you believe in, and what you think is most important in life. Is solitude especially good for that sort of pondering? Don't dismiss the little or mundane things, either. Is there something special about making your way through your everyday routines when you are on your own?

Let's take back our time alone! It is about sweet solitude, not just loneliness.

30.

Sweet Solitude: The Benefits It Brings, and the Special Strengths of the People Who Enjoy It

Here's what makes solitude so sweet

March 24, 2011 by Bella DePaulo, Ph.D. at Psychology Today

Unlike the readers of my last post, who were so articulate and insightful about the sweetness of solitude, many professional researchers have had a much harder time recognizing that solitude can actually be beneficial. Maybe part of the reason is that psychologists - especially social psychologists - are so attuned to humans as social animals who need and crave connection with other people. In fact, the title of a journal article that has attracted much attention over the years is "The need to belong."

I don't dispute the social needs of humans. I just don't see them as incompatible with an appreciation for solitude. To get a sense of psychologists struggling with the notion that time alone can actually be a GOOD thing, consider these two examples of titles of journal articles:

- "When the need to belong goes wrong"

- "Finding pleasure in solitary activities: desire for aloneness or disinterest in social contact?"

Titles such as these seem to suggest that if you spend time alone, there must be something wrong with you. Maybe your need to belong has "gone wrong." Maybe you don't really want to be alone, you are just anxious and avoiding other people. But that's not what the studies show. Some people really do want their time alone and regard it as something positive and constructive; they are not skittishly fleeing scary humans.

In a study of fifth through ninth graders, Reed Larson found that over time, the older children choose to spend more time alone. What's more, their emotional experience was improved after they had spent some time on their own. Those adolescents who spent an intermediate amount of time alone - not too much, not too little - seemed to be doing the best psychologically.

The psychologists who really do get it about the sweetness of solitude are the ones I mentioned in my last post - Christopher Long and James Averill. The title of their key theoretical article is "Solitude: An exploration of the benefits of being alone." No apology. No befuddlement that humans might actually benefit from their time alone.

Here's how they characterize solitude:

> "The paradigm experience of solitude is a state characterized by disengagement from the immediate demands of other people - a state of reduced social inhibition and increased freedom to select one's mental and physical activities."

Many readers made similar observations in the comments they posted to Part 1. Although there can be benefits to spending time with others, there can also be rewards to "disengagement from the immediate demands of other people."

There is research (again by Larson) in which people are beeped at random times during the day and asked about their experiences. Unsurprisingly, people report feeling less self-conscious when they are alone than when they are with others.

Other than the welcome emotional respite, what's so good about feeling less self-conscious? Long and Averill think that it is good for creativity. They note findings from other research showing that adolescents who can't deal with being alone are less likely to develop their creative abilities.

The theme that resonates most with me is the argument that other people can be distracting and taxing. I'm not talking specifically about being with people who are annoying and demanding. Instead, the idea is that just having other people around - even wonderful other people - can sap some of your cognitive and emotional resources. You might, even at some very low level, use up some of your psychological energy wondering about their needs and concerns, or considering the impression you may be making on them (even if you are not insecure about that), or maybe even just sensing their presence when you are sharing the same space and not even conversing.

There is a freedom that comes with solitude, and (as Long and Averill note) it is both a freedom from constraints and a positive freedom to do what you want and let your thoughts wander. Here's another quote from them that I especially appreciate, as it showcases their perspective that spending time alone and getting something out of it can be a strength, rather than a cause for concern:

> "the (positive) FREEDOM TO engage in a particular activity requires more than simply a FREEDOM FROM constraint or interference: it also requires the resources or capacity to use solitude constructively."

Antarctic researchers, who have chosen a pursuit that requires spending a lot of time alone, score especially high on a scale measuring "absorption." The scale assesses enjoyment of experiences such as watching clouds in the sky, and becoming particularly absorbed in a movie you are watching.

In solitude, Long and Averill suggest, we sometimes think about ourselves and our priorities in new ways. Our thinking about other matters, too, may be more likely to be transformed during times of solitude.

The particular intersection of solitude and single life - like so many other aspects of solitude - has yet to be studied in any detail. My guess is that people who are single - especially if they are single at heart - like their solitude more than people who crave coupling do. I'll end with one more quote from Long and Averill. They were not discussing single people when they said it, but it strikes me as relevant:

"...cognitive transformation can be threatening rather than liberating. At the very least, in order to benefit from solitude, the individual must be able to draw on inner resources to find meaning in a situation in which external supports are lacking."

References:

Long, C. R., & Averill, J. R. (2003). Solitude: An exploration of the benefits of being alone. JOURNAL FOR THE THEORY OF SOCIAL BEHAVIOR, 33, 21-44.

Larson, R. W. (1997). The emergence of solitude as a constructive domain of experience in early adolescence. *Child Development*, 68, 80-93.

31.

Alone: What Is It Good For?

The importance of the ability to be alone

April 22, 2012 by Bella DePaulo, Ph.D at PsychCentral

Much as Americans cherish rugged individualists in movies and novels and the lore of the pioneers, it has been a different story when it comes to everyday people living ordinary lives. Real people who live alone, and people who are single (regardless of whether they live on their own), are more often suspected than celebrated.

When I was researching *Singled Out*, I found that one of the most dogged myths about single people is that they are selfish and self-centered. It's not true – that's why I call it a myth – but it persists. How could single people, or solo dwellers, know how to sustain any kind of a relationship? How could they feel anything but loneliness? That's the old story.

Happily, a new perspective is emerging.

I have been interviewing people about how they live today. For example, do they live alone or with someone else? If alone, just how alone are they? If with others, who are those people and how do their lives intersect?

Toward the end of the interview, I ask participants to play the role of the sage, and dispense advice to other people about how to live. One person I interviewed, who has lived with other people and has lived alone, said this:

> "I think that unless people are comfortable living alone, they have trouble living with anyone else."

You may know the name Sherry Turkle from her most recent book, *Alone Together: Why We Expect More From Technology and Less From Each Other*. Just this weekend, Turkle, a psychology professor at M.I.T. who for decades has been studying the role of technology in our lives, also came out in favor of knowing how to be alone.

In an essay in the NEW YORK TIMES, she took on the ubiquity of texting and Twittering and Facebooking and checking our iPhones, even when we are with other people. (I seem to remember a NEW YORKER cartoon with a caption that said something like, "Let's all get together this weekend and stare at our iPhones.")

With our gush of quick tweets and truncated texts, she argues, we think we are connecting but what we are getting is not the full, rich experience of an actual conversation or meaningful interaction with another human. She thinks workplaces would be improved if a day a week were set aside for real conversations – no emailing or tweeting or texting allowed. In her own home, she has "device-free zones."

About our misunderstanding of aloneness and loneliness, she says this:

> "We think constant connection will make us feel less lonely. The opposite is true. If we are unable to be alone, we are far more likely to be lonely. If we don't teach our children to be alone, they will know only how to be lonely."

I like this hypothesis. As far as I know, though, it is just that. I would love to see some systematic research on the links among the ability to be alone, loneliness, skill at living with others, and the ability to forge and maintain genuine connections with other people.

32.

6 Psychological Insights about Solitude

There's a difference between pseudo-solitude and the real thing

February 19, 2014 by Bella DePaulo, Ph.D at PsychCentral

People who are single-at-heart love the time they have to themselves. In fact, when thinking about spending time alone, just about all of them react with something like, "Ah, sweet solitude," and almost none of them react with, "Oh, no, I might be lonely!"

With more and more people living single, and more and more people living alone, a better understanding of solitude is becoming increasingly important. Just recently, *The Handbook of Solitude* was published. I have a chapter in it, but in this post and the next I want to tell you about one of my favorite chapters, "Experiences of Solitude," by James Averill and Louise Sundararajan. It is a chapter that acknowledges the potential negative experiences of solitude, such as loneliness and boredom, but has far more to say about what can make solitude so sweet.

In Part 2, I'll tell you about the 20 different varieties of solitude experiences that they described. Here I want to share some of their other insights and suggestions.

#1 There is a difference between *authentic solitude*, in which the experience of being alone is mostly positive, and *pseudo-solitude*, which feels mostly like loneliness. Do you know what it is?

It's *choice*: "...authentic solitude is typically based on a decision to be alone; in contrast, pseudo-solitude, in which loneliness predominates, involves a sense of abandonment or unwanted isolation."

#2 Loneliness is not all negative. It can actually be part of an authentic solitude experience, as, for example, when people drift in and out of different feelings, including feelings of loneliness, when they are alone. Loneliness can also be motivating, as when it pushes people to figure out solutions to their problems. Only when loneliness dominates the experience of being alone and seems insurmountable does the experience get classified as pseudo-solitude.

#3 Do we appreciate solitude more as we grow older? I don't know of any definitive data on this, but the authors believe that we do, as did Einstein when he said, "I live in that solitude which is painful in youth, but delicious in years of maturity." Averill and Sundararajan believe that "the sentiment is true of many people of advanced age, who have learned to find solitude delicious but who are reluctant to admit the fact due to cultural prejudices."

#4 How can we understand how some people come to be good at being alone and others just can't handle it? Again, I don't know any great data on that, but the authors point to the 20th century psychoanalyst, Donald Winnocott, who believed that experiences during infancy are important. As the authors explained, "he posited that only those people who as infants were free to explore and independently occupy themselves in the security of their mothers' presence will as adults have the capacity to be alone." (Readers, do you have any ideas – or know of any research – on how people come to have the capacity to be alone? I'd love to hear from you if you do. Please share them in the comments section.)

#5 It is possible to experience solitude vicariously – for example, through art or poetry. Certain portrayals of nature can be especially effective.

#6 The kinds of opportunities we now have to experience solitude were largely missing in the past. "For example, in colonial America, young people were expected to establish a household as soon as they had the means to live independently. Within a household privacy was rarely possible, even in bed; and since households served multiple functions (educational, commercial, etc.), they were, in turn, under constant guidance and surveillance by the community."

I am so grateful to be living in a time when opportunities for solitude are abundant!

movies, bars, or the gym, she always has company. So she set out to try each of those activities, and more, on her own.

For me, a highlight of her restaurant experience was that when she walked into her neighborhood restaurant, she found that most of the other diners were…other people dining solo! I wish someone had been keeping track of restaurant diners over the years. I wonder whether, with the increase in the number of single people and the rise in people living alone and perhaps a lessening of self-consciousness in an era saturated with social media, the prospect of sitting in restaurants on your own is just not as daunting as it once was.

The reporter was not as eager to head out on her own as my students had been all those years ago. Like my students (and me), she learned something in the process. Here's how she describes one of her experiences going to a bar by herself:

> "Then into the bar came a woman who sat herself down next to me and opened a book and ordered dinner, all in one smooth move. She was by herself, but entirely unperturbed about that. She was the dining-alone person I wanted to be, effortlessly sipping her drink, underlining passages in her book, talking to the bartender — who eventually brought her a free dessert — and generally having the most wonderful of solo times, an outing that seemed even better because she was alone. She was alone not just for an experiment, not just because she was hungry, but because this was what she wanted to be doing, right here, right now.

> "I drank my wine and watched her and felt my alone endeavors pale in comparison to hers, until suddenly I realized I was doing exactly the same thing I'd feared others would do to me. I was judging **MYSELF**."

When *Singled Out* was first published in 2006, a reporter wanted to write a story about it for *Cosmo*. She talked to me at length, asked all the right questions, and tried and tried to pitch it. The editors could not be persuaded. So maybe something else has changed over time, and it is not just restaurant diners who are increasingly open to the solo experience.

36.

The Happy Loner

Should we be wary of loners or people who can't be alone?

June 24, 2014 by Bella DePaulo, Ph.D. at Psychology Today

"Loners" get a bad rap. "Loner" is the label we affix to criminals, outcasts, and just about everyone else we find scary or unsettling. In my all-time favorite book on the topic – *Party of One: The Loners' Manifesto* – author Anneli Rufus offers a whole different take on the true meaning of "loner." A loner, she says, is "someone who prefers to be alone." That person is so very different than all those who remain on the outside feeling isolated but so desperately wanted to be on the inside, feeling that they belong. The intense but thwarted craving for "acceptance, approval, coolness, companionship" is what sometimes sets off people who go ballistic on the objects of their desires.

In an essay in the GUARDIAN, Barbara Ellen lets us know that she has also had enough of the fear and the pity for people who actually LIKE their time alone. Here's how she opens her commentary:

> There used to be a fashion for scaremongering surveys about single women, saying things like: "8 out of 10 women are going to die alone, surrounded by 17 cats." But to that I would mentally add: "Or it could all go horribly wrong." To my mind, aloneness never necessarily equated with loneliness. It wasn't a negative, something to be avoided, feared or endured.

In the tradition of Anneli Rufus (and everyone else who recognizes that alone and lonely are not the same thing), Ellen knows that the kind of solitude that is chosen is a whole different experience than the type that is unwelcome. Riffing on a headline proclaiming that "Britain is the loneliness capital of Europe," Ellen offers an alternative perspective:

This study could just as well be interpreted as saying that many Britons are self-reliant problem-solvers, respectful of others people's privacy – and what's wrong with that? Isn't this the modern British definition of neighbourliness: not over-chummy and intrusive, but friendly, considerate and, most importantly, happy to sign for your Amazon parcels?

Barbara Ellen also poses a question that we should all ponder: Why is it that sociability is considered a skill, whereas the ability to be alone is seen as weird? As she notes:

Personally, I'd be more likely to distrust people who can't bear time with themselves. What's wrong with THEM that they can't abide their own company – what are they trying to hide in the crowd?

37.

Extraversion and the Single Person

Are single people more likely to be introverts?

January 2, 2011 by Bella DePaulo, Ph.D. at Psychology Today

Are people who stay single less extraverted than people who marry? That's a question that's been posed in the comments section of this blog a number of times. A relevant study suggests that the answer is: yes, probably.

Participants in the study were 6,876 Wisconsin adults, ages 53-54 and all non-Hispanic Whites. When they were first recruited, they were still in high school, but their extraversion was not measured until they were in their early 50s. So you can see the plusses and minuses of the study already - it is a big sample, but not a diverse one. It is a longitudinal study, but the key personality variable was only measured once, so we can't know how people's extraversion may have changed as they got married or unmarried or stayed single.

So here's what we do know: The 50-something year-olds who had stayed single were, on the average, less extraverted than their high school age mates who were married at the time of the testing. That was true of both the men and the women.

Two points to keep in mind: First, the introversion-extraversion dimension is different from social anxiety or shyness. The socially anxious are fearful about social interactions; introverts just prefer more time to themselves. Second, the author did not report the mean levels of extraversion for the different groups, so we can't know whether the singles were on the introverted end of the scale or just less extraverted than the marrieds.

I've often noted that it is inaccurate to say that single people are "alone" or that they don't have anyone. That's a myth. This study gives me the opportunity to emphasize a different point that is too often overlooked: Those singles who do spend more time on their own are not necessarily unhappy about that - in fact, many of them just may prefer it that way.

38.

The Living Arrangement That is the New Normal: Do You Know What It Is?

Is this the new standard of full adulthood?

November 14, 2010 by Bella DePaulo, Ph.D. at Psychology Today

Think about the many different living arrangements in the United States today. There is the nuclear family household, extended family households, pairs or groups of friends living together, and many more. Can you guess the living arrangement that is considered the new normal?

If you are not sure, let me offer a few hints:

- People who live in this type of household are mostly middle-aged

- It is a very stable household type

- People who live this way are often very social

The living arrangement that is the new normal is living solo. In fact, the BOSTON GLOBE article from which I drew the facts I just described is titled, "The new normal: living alone." It relates the work of sociologist Eric Klinenberg, and in a totally refreshing way. Instead of the doom and gloom that has characterized so many other articles on the rise of 1-person households, this story from a few days ago is very positive.

Three points that I especially appreciated were:

1. Klinenberg considers living solo to be "our emergent standard measure of full adulthood." Imagine that - what makes you an adult is not getting married but living on your own.

2. He also sees "living alone as a choice, not a form of exile."

3. Instead of moaning about all the lonely single people, the article ends with this quote from Klinenberg: "There's nothing lonelier than being in a bad marriage."

Other scholars, too, are recognizing the significance of the growing popularity of solo living, which extends far beyond the U.S. For instance, there is now a Solo-Living Research Network, with a webpage, membership page, and list of publications. Under "network aims," the first goal listed is "to share studies investigating the diversity of solo livers." That's promising, too. From the very outset, this group is recognizing that lots of different kinds of people live solo, and for many different reasons.

39.

Best Things about Living Alone — for People Who Mean It

There are profound reasons for wanting to live alone

August 23, 2014 by Bella DePaulo, Ph.D. at Psychology Today

Living alone is one of my things, so "best things about living alone" lists can lure me in the way most other listicles cannot. I've read lots of them. But here's the thing: I think they are for lightweights. And I think they are written by people who, deep down inside, do not really get it about the profound fulfillment of the solo-dwelling life. It's different for those of us who really mean it about wanting to live alone.

Consider the supposedly best things about living single as offered up by the lightweights from places such as *Cosmo* and *Buzzfeed*:

1. "You can use the bathroom without closing the door."

2. "You can stay up as long as you want. Without keeping it down for other people. Blast that episode of FRASIER!"

3. "Nobody will steal your food."

4. "You can leave your clothes on the floor…"

5. "You can do all the embarrassing and gross things you want without fear of judgment."

6. "…you don't ever have to wear pants."

7. "You don't have to worry about a roommate hearing you have sex, or vice versa."

8. "You never have to wait for anyone to get out of the bathroom to pee or shower."

9. "You can use all the hot water in the shower."

10. "You don't have to share the TV…"

All of these kinds of things are perfectly fine reasons for enjoying the experience of living alone. But if they are the ONLY kinds of reasons you like having a place of your own, then maybe you are not that serious about it. The reasons have a kind of defensiveness to them, as if you are trying to convince yourself that you really do like living alone. The reasons are mostly about freedom FROM constraints (you don't have to wear clothes, you don't have to share) and when they are about freedom TO DO things (stay up as long as you want), what is enabled by that freedom is trivial (watch reruns of FRASIER).

I like watching TV as much as the next person, but the freedom to do so is not among the most profound rewards of staying up as long as you want. Think about people who are really passionate about what they do. When they get engrossed in whatever it is that really grabs them – whether it is writing music or solving an intriguing problem or creating something or anything else – they love the freedom to just keep going. IT IS A JOY TO STAY ENGAGED, to go for hours without ever wondering about the time, to be free of concern about what some other person in the house thinks of you or wishes you were doing instead.

That's one of the real rewards of solo living for those who really mean it about wanting to live alone. Here are a few others:

- Other people are distracting and not just when they are talking to you or playing obnoxious music or watching annoying TV. The mere presence of other people can sap some of your emotional and intellectual resources. If someone else is around, a small part of you is paying attention to them. WHEN YOU LIVE ALONE, YOU CAN THINK WITH YOUR WHOLE MIND AND FEEL WITH YOUR WHOLE HEART.

- People who really mean it about wanting to live alone EXPERIENCE A SENSE OF APPRECIATION OF A PLACE OF THEIR OWN THAT IS BEYOND THE GRASP OF THE CAUSAL SOLO DWELLER. This is sometimes most apparent when they get their own place for the very first time. Even if the place is not all that great in objective ways (such as the size or the state of disrepair), people who crave living alone will savor and cherish it.

- For some people, living alone is not just a casual preference – it feels more like a need. What happens when you are deprived of a genuine need? You can't stop thinking about it. You daydream about it, makes plans for when you will get to have that need fulfilled again.

When living alone is a need and you finally get to do it after being deprived, YOU FEEL RELIEF AND A SENSE THAT YOUR LIVING SITUATION IS ONCE AGAIN JUST WHAT IT SHOULD BE.

VI.

Valuing Our Relationships –
Choosing to Spend Time with Others

40.

Are Single People More Independent or More Interconnected Than Married People?

The multi-faceted and stereotype-busting lives of single people

July 4, 2013 by Bella DePaulo, Ph.D at PsychCentral

Social scientists know what people think of singles, and often, it is not pretty. My colleagues and I did a series of studies to document perceptions and prejudices. In some studies, we asked people to tell us, in their own words, what came to mind when they thought about single (or married) people. In others, we created pairs of brief biographical sketches of people that were exactly the same except that in one of the sketches, the person was described as single, and in the other, as married. Then we asked participants to report their perceptions along a variety of dimensions.

Participants in our studies viewed single people more harshly than married people. They thought singles were less happy, less secure, lonelier, and more self-centered, among other disparaging traits. (They are wrong.) Yet one positive perception emerged in just about every study we ever did: Singles were seen as more independent than married people.S

In many ways, single people are often proud of their independence. Single people who are single-at-heart love having time and space to themselves, and they like making their own decisions. Unsingle people sometimes envy the independence they ascribe to people who are single.

When so many other perceptions of single people are negative, I guess I should embrace the positive perception of independence. Yet in some ways, it troubles me. Too often, others believe that singles are independent in the dubious sense of having no ties to other people. One version of this is the myth that single people "don't have anyone." Another is that singles are free of all caretaking responsibilities.

The irony of these perceptions is that in some senses, they are exactly wrong. When people, such as aging parents, are in need of long-term care, often it is the single people who are expected to step in and provide it, and the single people who actually do rearrange their own lives to help others who cannot help themselves. Yet single people do not have a spouse whose salary can cover both of them plus the person in need of help. Financially, they are often more vulnerable than married people when they try to do intensive caregiving and maintain their source of income as well.

In everyday life, too, single people are more connected to other people than our stereotypes would lead us to believe, and more connected than married people are. For starters, most single people do not live alone. In the U.S., for example, there are more than 100 million unmarried adults 18 and older, but only about 33 million people live alone.

Single people are also more likely than married people to maintain ties and exchange help with neighbors, friends, siblings, and parents. In longitudinal studies, in which people are followed over time, those who get married become more insular; they are less likely to stay in touch with other people than they were when they were single. That does not change with time, unless they get divorced – then they once again become more attentive to others.

The results of all of these big studies are averages. That means that the results do not characterize all single people or all married people. Yet by now, there are quite a few studies of connectedness and caring among single and married people, and they are quite consistent in suggesting that, typically, it is single people who are doing more to foster family (beyond the nuclear) and community.

I think that many (though not all) couples practice what I call "intensive coupling." They look to their partner to be their everything – what I called, in *Singled Out*, Seepies: Sex and Everything Else Partners. When things are going great in a romantic relationship, intensive coupling can be fine. For some, it may even seem glorious. Yet when a relationship hits the skids, what happens to the two people who relegated all of the other people in their lives to the back burner?

Again, there are many exceptions, but I think that in general, single people are more likely to maintain a diversified relationship portfolio. They don't invest all of their relationship capital into just one person.

The answer to the question posed by the title of this article, "Are single people more independent or more interconnected than married people," is both.

41.

Who Is Your Family If You Are Single with No Kids?

Yes, you do have a family

August 21, 2011 by Bella DePaulo, Ph.D. at Psychology Today

There is an implied question behind the question, "Single, no children: Who is your family?" That lurking query is, do you even have a family? The first answer is yes. Singles with no children, just like married people and parents, have families of origin. They may have nuclear family members - parents, brothers, and sisters - and extended family members such as grandparents, aunts, uncles, cousins, siblings-in-law, nieces and nephews.

Once upon a time, "family" seemed to be comprised of sturdy and immovable parts. Scholars had a name for the family they most often studied and wrote about: "Standard North American Family." Now, hardly anything about family seems standard or obligatory. According to a number of academic and bureaucratic (e.g., the Census Bureau) definitions, families do not need to include children (couples count); they do not need to include more than one adult and they do not need to include two people in a sexual relationship (single-parent families count); when they do include two adults, those adults do not need to be married (cohabiting couples count) and they do not need to include a man and a woman (same-sex couples count). To count as family, the members do not even need to live under the same roof (there are commuter marriages and "living apart together" arrangements, there are divorced families that extend across households, and immigrant families that reach across nations).

Setting aside families of origin, perhaps what distinguishes the families of singles with no children from other families is that typically just one person stands at the center. Other family forms begin with a couple, a parent-child dyad, or a nuclear family unit. Perhaps that difference is partly to blame for the popular misconception (DePaulo, 2006) that single people with no children "don't have anyone": They don't have a spouse or spouse-equivalent, and in later life, they will have no grown children. They don't have someone with the same sense of obligation to care for them as do people in the other family forms. Left unanalyzed, that conceptualization can foster fear among singles, and fuel the myths that many accept as truth. A fake person, Bridget

Jones, probably said it best. Stereotypically, singles will end up "dying alone and found three weeks later half-eaten by an Alsatian" (Fielding, 1996).

I have argued that we should NOT set aside families of origin. Singles with no children who have living parents or siblings DO have people in their lives who may love them, care about them, and feel obligated to be there for them.

What I have also done in this chapter is to ask not (just) who is obligated to help, but who really does help? Who does all of the things that families - in the ideal case -- typically do? What I showed by reviewing the literature is that singles with no children do family-type things. They care for those who cannot care for themselves; socialize the young; share experiences and create a sense of continuity and identity; and exchange emotional, practical, and material support.

In fact, in some ways, singles reliably do more than their share. When people who have always been single are compared to the previously married and the currently married in the extent to which they exchange social and instrumental support, provide care, and stay in touch with people such as parents, siblings, friends, and neighbors, it is the currently married people who are nearly always at the bottom of the list. That's why the contemporary institution is sometimes called "greedy marriage." In the United States, many married couples and nuclear families turn inward, expecting undivided commitment to one another.

That expectation and the accompanying feeling of obligation contribute to the sense that people who are married "have someone." When all is well, they do. What is less often considered is what happens when the relationship is in trouble, or when one partner is facing a grave challenge such as a serious illness. Who will step in to help then? The risks are that no one else will know that help is needed or will feel close enough to offer that help; or that others will regard the matters as private or will assume that because each member of the couple already "has someone," they do not need help from anyone else. Many of these kinds of dynamics are in need of further research attention.

People who have children sometimes feel confident that in later life, they will be in a better position than those who never did have children. Their grown children, they believe, will be there for them when needed. In fact, however, grown children may turn out to be emotionally or geographically distant, preoccupied with their own lives, or otherwise disengaged and unhelpful. Research on widowed parents and their grown children (Ha & Carr, 2005) has shown that when the widows live near or with their adult children, there can be benefits. For example, they experience less psychological distress than when their children are far away. However, that emotional comfort does

NOT occur - and can even be undermined - when the widowed parents feel overly dependent on their grown children. When the parents live with their adult children and not just nearby, their own social world shrinks - they spend substantially less time with friends, relatives, and neighbors.

Another approach to studying family-type relationships in the lives of singles with no children is to drop the family terminology entirely and simply ask people to name the most important people in their lives or to map those people onto concentric circles. The personal communities that are described by this methodology are sometimes restricted ones, with perhaps just one person in the innermost circle. Such limited personal communities tend to leave people psychologically vulnerable, regardless of their marital or parental status. Among the personal communities that are not restricted, some are more family-oriented and others more friends-oriented. Communities in which friends are well-represented (even in the absence of family) are more protective of psychological well-being than are communities in which family is well-represented (in the absence of friends). Single women with no children are particularly likely to have friend-based personal communities.

For decades, Western societies have been changing in ways that are bringing single adults and adults with no children to the forefront. Yet there is little consideration of what family means to singles with no children. When participants in national surveys (such as the Pew surveys) are asked whether various sets of people count as family, the kinds of living arrangements relevant to singles with no children are not even represented.

That is likely to change. Scholars such as Barry Wellman who have studied changes in social networks over time and around the globe argue that "in some societies, there may be a turn away from the household to the individual as the basic personal networking unit" (Wellman, 2007). The phenomenon is called "networked individualism." Although singles living solo are especially likely to fit that description, others qualify too. To quote Wellman (2007) again, "The emerging picture is of 'networked individuals' operating somewhat autonomously out of 'networked households' (Wellman, 2001; Kennedy and Wellman, 2007)." Even in contemporary nuclear families, experiences are not shared as much as they once were. Instead, individual family members sit in front of their own computers surfing their own favorite sites, watching their own preferred shows, and communicating with their own friends. There are individual cell phones rather than a family phone, and individual cars in families who can afford them. For married couples, the evidence is not just anecdotal. A study comparing couples in the year 2000 to those from 20 years previously showed that the couples from 2000 were less likely than the ones from 1980 to work on projects around the house together, go out together, visit friends together, or even to eat together (Amato, Booth, Johnson, & Rogers, 2007).

In the opening years of the 21st century, we are still accustomed to asking people about their families. Maybe in the decades to come, it will not be just the phone companies who instead ask, "Who's in your network?"

42.

If You Are Single, Will You Grow Old Alone? Results from 6 Nations
Are singles with no kids isolated and vulnerable in later life?

January 19, 2011 by Bella DePaulo, Ph.D. at Psychology Today

You know the scare story - if you are single, you will grow old alone. I'll take that scare story and raise it - if you are single and have no children, you will surely grow old alone. Not!

Scholars have been remiss in mostly neglecting the study of adults who have no children, and especially, within that category, adults who have always been single. Within the past few years, though, a wonderful collection of datasets from as many as 9 different countries has begun to be mined. The participating scholars have looked into all sorts of questions about adults with no children. Here, I'd like to tell you what they've learned about the social support networks of older people who have always been single and have no children.

Complete information on social networks could be culled from six of the countries:

- Australia
- Finland
- The Netherlands
- Spain
- The UK
- The US

All of the participants were at least 65 years old. The key question that motivated the authors was whether these older people, who had been single all their lives and had no children, would have the kinds of restrictive social support networks that would leave them vulnerable in their later lives. For each country, the authors compared 12 groups: men without children, women without children, mothers and fathers - and within those groups, people who had always been single or were currently married or were previously married.

Five different kinds of social support networks were identified. The first two are the most limited:

1.   LOCAL SELF-CONTAINED: people with this type of network are mostly home-centered in their lives, reaching out to neighbors when necessary.

2.   PRIVATE RESTRICTED: this very limited support network is typical of married couples who mostly look only to each other for support, only rarely connecting with locals for help.

Less restricted than the first two are:

3.   LOCAL FAMILY DEPENDENT: people with these networks have relatives nearby and they rely on them when they need help or support.

In the last two types of social support networks, friends have important roles and other people do, too.

4.   LOCALLY INTEGRATED: people with these networks have kin nearby who are part of their social networks, but friends and neighbors are also important to them.

5.   WIDER COMMUNITY FOCUSED: People with these networks have no relatives nearby, though if they do have kin, they stay in touch with them. Their social support networks include friends and members of local voluntary groups.

As you might imagine, with 6 different countries and 12 kinds of marital/parental groups and 5 types of social networks, the results can be complex. Still, amidst all of the details, some telling patterns did emerge. Two of them characterize all of the countries except Australia (which I'll discuss later).

First, adults with no children tended to have the most restricted networks - either local self-contained or private restricted.

Second, there was a big exception to the first conclusion. Women who had always been single and who had no children often had the kinds of support networks in which friends were important - either locally integrated networks (in which local kin and neighbors, as well as friends, were part of the everyday support system) or wider community focused networks (among those who had no relatives nearby).

In Australia, both the men and the women who had always been single were likely to have local self-contained networks. Among the other marital/parental groups, the wider community focused network was much more commonplace than it was in the other countries. The authors speculate that the huge size of the country, together with the low population density, may contribute to different results for Australians, but they don't really know for sure.

So are they vulnerable - those adults in later life who have always been single and have no children? The men in that category are more likely to have restricted networks than men in most other categories. Even for them, though, the vast majority of them (except in Australia) have support networks that are not restricted. Specifically, the **percentages** of always-single men with no children who have local self-contained networks are specified in the first number in the list below. (I'll explain the second later.)

%

59 for Australia (vs. 9)

31 for Finland (vs. 61)

28 for the Netherlands (vs. 36)

 0 for Spain (vs. 18)

17 for the UK (vs. 43)

16 for the US. (vs. 30)

The second number for each nation is the percentage of married men with no children who have private restricted networks. These men mostly rely on their spouse and no one else. That's a kind of vulnerability, too.

For the always-single women with no children, the answer to the question of whether they are growing old alone is a resounding no. They are especially likely to have locally integrated or wider community focused social support networks.

Reference:

Wenger, G. C., Dykstra, P. A., Melkas, T., & Knipscheer, K. C. P. M. (2007). Social embeddedness and late-life parenthood: Community activity, close ties, and support networks. JOURNAL OF FAMILY ISSUES, 11, 1419-1456.

43.

Aging on Your Own: 5 Things You May Not Know

The scare stories are myths

July 20, 2012 by Bella DePaulo, Ph.D at PsychCentral

Oh, to be old and on your own. That used to be one of the media's favorite scare stories. To some extent, it still is. The reality, though, is a whole lot different. Over the past half-century or so, what it means to be aging on your own has been changing dramatically – in many ways, for the better.

The Council on Contemporary Families (CCF) released a report called "Aging alone in America." It was written by Eric Klinenberg (you know him from his *Going Solo* book), Stacy Torres, and Elena Portacolone.

Here are some of questions and conclusions from the CCF report.

#1. Why are more older Americans on their own? It is not just about women outliving their husbands.

If the educated layperson knows one thing about the demographics of aging, it is that women live longer than men and so in later life, the women who have outlived their husbands are often living on their own. That's true. And, of course, some Americans are on their own in later life because they never did marry.

There's another factor, too, and this one was news to me. I have been hearing for a long time that the divorce rate has leveled off – it is no longer increasing. What I didn't know was how different the numbers are by age. From the CCF report:

"While divorce rates have fallen for younger Americans over the past 30 years, THE DIVORCE RATE FOR PEOPLE OVER 65 HAS DOUBLED SINCE 1990." [emphasis mine]

#2. But why are they LIVING alone?

Just because you are widowed or divorced or have always been single does not mean that you are living on your own – in your own place, shared by no one else. Increasingly, though, more and more older Americans are living just that way.

Consider, for example, this striking reversal, as described in the CCF report:

> "One hundred years ago, 70 percent of American widows and widowers moved in with their families. Today nearly the same proportion of widows and widowers live alone."

Why the change? Because it is what older people want. Staying in their own places – now called "aging in place" – is their first choice of how to live. That is so even when their grown kids want to take them in, a willingness that has actually increased in the most recent generation.

#3. Money is the enabler and the disabler.

There is another crucial reason why more seniors are living on their own – they can afford to. The poverty rate among the elderly had fallen dramatically over time. Thank-you, Social Security. Thank-you, Medicare.

Of course, when it comes to economic resources, not all seniors are equal. Here are some groups especially likely to struggle financially in later life:

1. Financially, aging RENTERS have a harder time than aging homeowners. But even those who have fully paid for the homes that they own still have to pay property taxes and cover any maintenance and repair expenses that come up.

2. Older WOMEN are more likely to be living in poverty than older men, 10.7 percent compared to 6.6 percent.

3. BLACK and HISPANIC women who live alone are particularly likely to be poor, 38 percent and 41 percent, respectively.

#4. Nora Ephron may have felt badly about her neck**, but other body parts are not what we expect**.

If you live alone and you have serious health problems, that will be difficult. No sugar coating. But the odds of that happening are actually dropping. Again, from the CCF report:

"Disability rate have been falling. And a 2009 Pew Research Center survey found that the percentage of young and middle-aged adult who expected to experience problems associated with old age such as memory loss, serious illness, or lack of sexual activity was much higher than the percentage of older adults who reported actually dealing with these issues."

#5. In *Singled Out*, **I made fun of the myth that "you will grow old alone and you will die in a room by yourself where no one will find you for weeks." The CCF report agrees that many of these scare stories are myths**.

I have often discussed the studies showing that people who are single are more often in touch with other people such as friends and neighbors, compared to those who are married. The CCF report underscores that the same is true if you look just at the older people who are living alone.

Women, especially, seem to do well on their own in later life:

> "A 2007 study funded by the Economic and Social Research Council found that women over sixty who lived alone expressed more happiness with their lives than married women of the same age."

44.

Who Keeps Siblings Together When They Become Adults?

Single people provide the glue that keeps siblings together

November 16, 2010 by Bella DePaulo, Ph.D. at Psychology Today

One of the raps on single people is that they create alienation and anomie. A nation that would be connected, family-oriented, and community-minded if all those singles were married instead becomes a nation of isolates because of all the people living single.

I've often mentioned a set of studies that suggests quite the opposite. People who have always been single are more likely than currently married people (especially) or previously married people (to a lesser extent) to help, encourage, visit, and communicate with friends, neighbors, siblings, and parents. That's what Naomi Gerstel and Natalia Sarkisian found in their paper titled "Marriage: the good, the bad, and the greedy." The data relevant to sibling relationships came from the 1992-1994 National Survey of Families and Households. That's a nationally representative sample, so that's the good part. However, the analyses were from just one point in time. So, it was not possible to know for sure that the married people were less often in touch with their siblings BECAUSE they got married or that the previously married people tended to maintain more contact with their sibs than currently married people did BECAUSE they got unmarried.

As I continue to research my chapter on the place of family in the lives of people who are single with no children, I've been trying to learn more about siblings. I found a report of an earlier wave of that National Survey of Families and Households, from 1987-1988. Once again, results showed that people who had a spouse or partner were less likely to visit or call or write to their siblings than were those who were single. Again, though, the data were from just one point in time.

Happily, sociologist Lynn White has studied the changes in contact with siblings between the 1978-1988 survey and the 1992-1994 data collection. Following the same people over time, did those who got married have less contact with their sibs than they did before, and did people who got divorced have more contact? The answer to both questions is yes (from Table 3, if you can access the article).

To answer the question in the title of this post, the people who provide the glue to sibling relationships in adult life are those who are single. People who have always been single are especially good at this, but the previously married also do better than the currently married.

You can probably guess the matrimaniacal explanation that is sometimes offered for findings like this (it also comes up in discussions of singles and their pets) - single people are just "compensating" for not having a spouse. By that way of thinking, single people don't really value their siblings (or their parents or the friends or neighbors they stay in touch with more than currently married people do) - those other people are just consolation prizes.

Gerstel and Sarkisian's "greedy marriage" explanation is different. Discussing married people's weaker ties to siblings, parents, neighbors, and friends, the scholars note that marriage can "demand a kind of intense emotional involvement that by itself detracts from collective life...Finding a soul mate means turning inward - pushing aside other relationships."

They are quick to note, though, that greediness is not intrinsic to marriage. Instead, it seems to be a by-product of the intensive way that marriage and coupling is practiced in contemporary American society. I would also add that there are differences from one married person to another in the degree to which they regard their partner as the near-exclusive focus of their adult social life.

Compared to spouses and romantic partners, adult siblings get little attention from academics. By their neglect, scholars are enabling the clueless question often posed to people known to have siblings: Do you have a family?

45.

If You Are Single, Is Every Day Independence Day?

Test your knowledge of independence and interdependence

July 4, 2013 by Bella DePaulo, Ph.D. at Psychology Today

Is it true that single people are especially likely to value their independence? Are they especially likely to savor solitude? Does independence imply a lack of connection with other people?

Take the quick quiz below to test your knowledge of single-people's independence and interdependence. All of the quiz answers are based on research. All of the answers are at the end. The links within each question take you to a discussion of the research results.

Apologies to regular readers of this blog, for whom this quiz is likely to be way too easy.

#1 When a family member such as an aging parent becomes seriously ill and needs lots of care, who is most often expected to provide that care?

> A. The grown child who is single
> B. The grown child who is married

#2 When someone is sick, disabled, or elderly and in need of care for at least three months, who is more likely to actually provide that care?

> A. Single people
> B. Married people

#3 Who is more likely to provide help to friends, neighbors, and coworkers by providing a ride when needed, doing shopping or other errands?

> A. Single people

> B. Married people

#4 Who is more likely to help friends and neighbors with housework, yard work, repairs, or other work around the house?

> A. Single people

> B. Married people

#5 Who is more likely to provide advice, encouragement, and moral or emotional support to friends, neighbors, siblings, and parents?

   A. Single people

   B. Married people

#6 Who is more likely to maintain ties with siblings?

   A. People who stay single or get divorced

   B. People who get married

#7 TRUE OR FALSE: When people first get married, they spend less time with their friends and maintain less contact with their parents than they did when they were single, but that's just a newlywed effect – within a few years, their connections with their friends and parents are just as frequent as they were before.

#8 TRUE OR FALSE: Any tendency among married people to focus less on friends, neighbors, parents, and siblings is just a White thing; it does not happen among African-Americans or Hispanics.

#9 Who is especially likely to savor their time to themselves?

   A. People who are single at heart

   B. People who are not single at heart

#10 Who is more likely to want to make big decisions mostly on their own?

   A. People who are single at heart

   B. People who are not single at heart

#11 Who is more likely to prefer handling challenges on their own?

   A. People who are single at heart

   B. People who are not single at heart

#12 How do most single people live?

   A. Most single people live alone

   B. Most single people live with other people

Answers: The answers to both True/False questions (7 & 8) are False. The answer to the last question (12) is **B**. The answer to all other questions is **A**.

46.

Singles or Couples: Who Has More Confidants? More Diverse Confidants?

No one to talk to? Here's the latest

August 12, 2010 by Bella DePaulo, Ph.D. at Psychology Today

Recently, on my personal blog, I made fun of a CNN columnist for suggesting that "acting single" means that you don't talk to anyone about what's going on in your life. The article struck me as a variation on the discredited stereotype that single people are alone and don't have anyone.

Now I can add even more myth-busting data to that bit of singles-bashing. In a study that is in press in the journal INFORMATION, COMMUNICATION, & SOCIETY, Keith Hampton and his colleagues asked 2,152 Americans to answer this question:

"From time to time, most people discuss important matters with other people. Looking back over the last six months, who are the people with whom you discussed matters that are important to you?"

On the average, the participants named about two people in response to this question about their confidants. Who named more, the singles or the couples? (Couples were people who were married or living with a partner.)

Neither. Singles and couples had the same number of people with whom they had discussed important matters. Each coupled person had someone right there under the same roof as a potential confidant. At least in comparison to singles living on their own, you might think they had a head start on their current list of confidants. But they end up, on the average, with the same number.

There are many potential ways to assess the diversity of a person's set of confidants. One of the approaches the authors used was to look at whether all of the confidants were some sort of family member (parent, sibling, child, spouse, or other relative) or whether other kinds of people (such as friends) were included too.

So who was more likely to have a set of confidants that included people in addition to kin? The singles were.

Here I will add my predictable disclaimer: To understand these findings better, I'd like to see a longitudinal study. As people become coupled, do they ditch or demote their friends and start confiding only to their partner and other family members? Or are the kinds of people who become partnered less likely to confide in friends from the outset? Or is this focus on the family something about the people who are left in the coupled group after all of those who got married and then got unmarried are set aside?

The study was not designed as a test of the link between marital status and confidants. I found the relevant data in the tables that were included in the article. Instead, the authors were pursuing the finding that sent the American media into paroxysms of panic a few summers ago - the claim that 21st century Americans were dramatically less likely to have confidants than they were in the mid-80s. They add some intriguing new findings and insights to that discussion. I'll get to those in a later post.

Reference:
Hampton, K. N., Sessions, L. F., & Ja Her, E. (in press). Core networks, social isolation, and new media: Internet and mobile phone use, network size, and diversity. Information, Communication, & Society.

47.

The Meaning of 'Relationship': Notes from a Party

What relationship scholars don't seem to know about relationships

March 13, 2010 by Bella DePaulo, Ph.D. at Psychology Today

Yesterday, I listened to an eminent relationship scholar talk about the research he has been conducting for decades. It is great work, and the talk was impressive. Except for one thing: When he talked about "relationships," he was actually referring to just one kind of relationship - a romantic one.

In our everyday conversations, we often use the word "relationship" in that one specific way. So when you ask someone whether they are in a relationship, they will answer "no" as long as they are not in a coupled relationship.

"Relationship," though is a great big word. It covers all sorts of human connections, including ties to friends, parents, children, siblings, other family members, coworkers, neighbors, mentors, and more.

There is a lively academic field of personal relationships, complete with multiple journals, annual conferences, funded research projects, and stacks of books. Asked for a formal definition of "relationship," no scholar would limit the description only to connections that might include sex. Yet, that's how academics use the word in their talks and even in their scholarly publications.

Articles published in relationship-relevant journals have titles such as these:

- "Theories of relationships"

- "Reciprocity in relationships"

- "Aspects of interpersonal relationships"

- "Relationship quality and self-other concepts"

Yet these articles, and many others like them, aren't actually about relationships, in the big, broad, accurate sense of the word; they are only about couples' relationships.

Decades ago, when scholars did studies that included (say) only men, they could publish titles and summaries that referred to people in general, giving readers the impression that their research was about all of humanity. Only when readers got to the methods section would they realize that there were no women included in the research. These days, that's not allowed. First, unless you are studying something like prostate cancer, you can't include only men in your research and still get federal funding. Second, if you have a compelling reason to study just one group, you need to acknowledge that limitation in the abstract (summary). It is time for relationship researchers to do the same.

There's something much more troubling than the use of the word "relationship" in a way that excludes all relationship types except one. All of the other adult relationships are not just excluded in the wording, they are absent from the studies.

In 2002, Karen Fingerman and Elizabeth Hay searched through all of the articles published over the course of six years in the six academic journals that most often publish relationship-relevant research. They found 976 relevant studies. Then, for each relationship type, they counted the number of studies that included that relationship. Here I'll highlight the findings that show the contrast in attention paid to couples' relationships compared to other adult relationships (there were other results in addition to these):

- 432 studies of spouses

- 245 studies of romantic partners

- 12 studies of best friends

- 124 studies of friends

- 40 studies of siblings

The field of adult relationships research is dominated by the study of coupled relationships. Yet, if you were to ask people, all through their adult lives, if they have a romantic partner, a friend, or a sibling, you would find at every age that more people have a friend and more have a sibling than have a spouse or partner.

When I first wrote about the Fingerman and Hay study for this post, I did it from memory (except for looking up the exact numbers), since it is a study I've talked about many times before. Then when I searched for a link to include here, I reread the abstract and was reminded of something else that seems significant. In a second study, the authors asked relationship scholars and other people without advanced degrees to indicate how important they thought various kinds of relationships were. They found that "less-educated individuals rated many social ties as more important than did researchers who study relationships." Interesting, isn't it?

If you were to open the various child development journals and shake out all of the relationship research, you would be buried in an avalanche of studies of children's friendships. But among the scholars of adult relationships, it is as if they have decided that friends are for kids.

At a party held after the talk, as I was holding forth about how we should not use the word relationship to refer only to coupled relationships, an Asian scholar pointed out that the American obsession with the couple relationship is hardly universal. Where she grew up, it is the mother-child bond that is most central. Then another question was raised: Why is it that academics studying relationships have focused so overwhelmingly on couples' relationships? I don't know the answer, and will save my guesses for some other time.

For now, my bottom line is this: If you have a friend, a sibling, a parent, a child, a cousin, a coworker, a neighbor, or just about any other person in your life, and you maintain a connection with that person, you have a relationship. You are IN a relationship.

I feel the same way about love. It is a word with big, broad meanings. Let's celebrate all of them.

48.

Bigger, Broader Meanings of Love and Romance

Soulmates? Love and romance come in so many more varieties

May 11, 2008 by Bella DePaulo, Ph.D. at Psychology Today

A few weeks ago, Ted Sorensen - husband, father, and renowned speechwriter for President John F. Kennedy - was interviewed by the New York Times. Consider this excerpt:

> *NY Times*: "Was your working relationship with J.F.K. the great love affair of your life?"

> *Sorensen*: "Yes, of course."

A public figure, a married man, says to the paper of record that the great love affair of his life was not with his wife but with his boss, the President.

Ted Sorensen is not listening to the music. Lyrics such as "You're my everything;" "I just want to be your everything;" and "How do I live without you?...You're my world, my heart, my soul" express the myth of modern marriage: Find "The One" and your whole life falls into place. No pursuit, no passion, no love could be any greater than the love you feel when you finally embrace your soulmate - not music, not scientific discovery, and surely not speechwriting.

To many Americans, the soulmate interpretation of love is not an interpretation, it is not a myth, and it is not modern. Rather, it is The Way It Is, and the way it always has been. I think I believed something like that myself, before I started doing the research for Singled Out. It didn't make any sense for me to believe in the soulmate mythology, since I have always been single, I've always loved my single life (well, except for the singlism and the matrimania), and I have never had any desire to become unsingle. Still, I figured I was the exception.

In my high school, history was taught by the athletic coaches, so we learned mostly about the history of the scoring that took place in the game the night before. I realized how woefully unprepared I was to take a real history course when I got to college, so I didn't. Those were the days when there were hardly any requirements. I took 19 psychology courses.

Once I started reading social history, all these years later, I was amazed at what I had missed. From Francesca Cancian's Love in America, I learned that less than a century before the married couple and their feelings for each other had become so glorified, "intimacy and sexual relations between spouses were NOT central and both spouses had important ties with relatives and friends of their own sex."

In Marriage, A History, Stephanie Coontz noted that during the 1800s, Westerners believed that "love developed slowly out of admiration, respect, and appreciation;" therefore, "the love one felt for a sweetheart was not seen as qualitatively different from the feeling one might have for a sister, a friend, or even an idea."

I don't think Americans have lost the bigger, broader senses of love and romance and passion and meaning that have probably been part of the human experience through the ages. Rather, I think that contemporary American society has been slow to give those experiences their due. It is ordinary, nowadays, to express one's love and devotion to a life partner. It is far from ordinary to do as Sorensen did and proclaim his life's work to be the great love affair of his life.

I've taken to gathering unabashed expressions of dedication to something or someone other than a soulmate. Here's a sampling from my collection.

In 2004, singer and songwriter John Mayer told Newsweek: "I really might just be the guy who loves playing music so much that [even] if I'm on a date with somebody, I can't wait to go home and play guitar. If I even seal the deal, I can't wait for them to leave so I can play the guitar."

Sometimes book titles say it all. The Man Who Loved Only Numbers, for instance, is about the brilliant mathematician Paul Erdos, who spend decades "crisscrossing four continents, chasing mathematical problems in pursuit of lasting beauty and ultimate truth."

The title Liberty, A Better Husband comes from the diary of Louisa May Alcott. The author was writing about the single woman of antebellum America, who "envisioned her liberty as both autonomy and affiliation...Her freedom enabled her to commit her life and her capacities to the betterment of her sex, her community, or her kin."

For generations of women and men devoted to the cause of social justice, the meanings of love and passion have always transcended diamond rings and limestone altars.

Of course, Ted Sorensen, John Mayer, Paul Erdos, and Louisa May Alcott are in the stratospheres of their fields. That's not a requirement. Love and romance and meaning can be found in everyday life. In her book, The New Single Woman, Kay Trimberger described one woman's passion for flamenco dancing. A whole book full of tributes to big, broad meanings of love is what you will find in Isn't It Romantic? Finding the Magic in Everyday Life. Examples range from the love of nature and architecture to the "the romance of perfect solitude" and the weaving and cherishing of a "web of silver strings" between a Juilliard teacher of song and her vulnerable students.

There's a special place in my collection for the pairs of people who have said the following about one another: "We fell in love." "We are planning a future together." "We use the exact same expressions, sighs, and body language without realizing it, often at the same time." We are "memory banks for each other." All are quotes from friends, not lovers.

Here's one last example. This one comes from a woman writing about the appeal of working alone in her office at home:

> "There I am drawn to the warm southern exposure, the familiarity of my papers strewn everywhere, piles on the bed, the floor, the desk. Mostly, I'm drawn to the stillness. The only sound is the muted hum of the computer. I've dreamed of a room like this for years but never imagined how comforting it would feel to walk in every day."

The person who wrote this was married, but was craving a sabbatical from her marriage. What she really wanted, at least for a while, was to be single. Now THAT's romantic!

VII.

Sex and the Single Person: Have It Your Way – Or Just Skip It

49.

Sex and the Single Person

Myths about the sex lives of singles

May 25, 2009 by Bella DePaulo, Ph.D. at Psychology Today

Over the course of history, the "shoulds" and "should-nots" of sex have changed dramatically. There have been times when sex was not discussed in polite company, times when women were believed merely to tolerate the experience, times when engaging in sex before marriage was considered scandalous, and many other permutations as well. Now the should-scale has tipped in another direction. We are all - women and men, both - expected to want and crave sex, lots of it, whether we are married or single or in some unclassifiable state in between. During each historical era, the prevailing view seemed natural and true.

In her widely-read essay, "Sex is not a natural act," Leonore Tiefer put it this way:

> "The modern view of sexuality as a fundamental drive that is very individualized, deeply gendered, central to personality and intimate relationships, separate from reproduction, and lifelong (literally womb-to-tomb) would be quite unrecognizable to people living in different civilizations."

The desires of many contemporaries do, in fact, conform to today's new sex-suffused norm. Theirs is not a forced fit but a genuine one. For those who not only like lots of sex but can readily find compatible partners, these are the best of times. (Although, with AIDS still unconquered, these are also among the riskiest of times.)

The dark side of the new norms, though, is that they leave little room for people with different sexual profiles or opportunities. For those would like to have a sexual relationship but don't, the relentless celebration of all things sexual must be particularly painful. (Thanks to commenter Incel for reminding me to acknowledge the community of Involuntary Celibates. You can read more in Chapter 9 of A History of Celibacy.) Those who simply care less - or not at all - about sex are marginalized by contemporary sexual norms, too. In other eras, they may have felt virtuous. Now, even the most contented among them must wonder at times whether there is something wrong with them.

The relentless feting of sex and the implacable sexualizing of society has shaped and strengthened a particular stereotype of singles - that their lives, more than those of married people - are driven by sex. Singles, it is believed, are always looking for sex but not finding it, or indulging in too much of it for their own good, or they are spectacularly bad at it, or they are such cold fish that they could never enjoy it, or - well, think of something damning, and it has probably been said about singles. All of those criticisms really are true of some singles. But here's the point: They are also true of some married people. And as a generalization, mindlessly applied to a whole swatch of people, not one of the caricatures is accurate.

When it comes to sex, people who are single have been set up. The group to whom they are compared does not consist of real married people but idealized ones. In the matrimaniacal picture in our minds, married people - simply because they are married - have magical access to perfect sex. One spouse's wish is the other's desire. A partner is always there, willing and able, never too tired, never not in the mood. Each spouse wants just the same amount and kind of sex as the other, and at exactly the same times.

Of course, if that were true, a lot of marriage counselors would be out of a job.

So yes, there are challenges around sex for people who are single. But do not believe for a split second that getting married will make all of your sexual dreams come true. Sure, there can be tremendous rewards for partners who are sexually compatible and who stay that way for the duration. But if and when things fall apart - as one person wants more sex and the other wants less, as one wants to experiment and the other is appalled by the mere thought of it, as one or both become bored or even hostile - being married can be even more daunting than being single. Especially if there are children involved. Any two people, married or not, can work on their relationship and their sex, and get counseling if they are so inclined, but when all efforts prove futile, married people are entangled in a way that singles are not.

It is not even true that getting married means that your sexual experiences will become less risky. A review of all available research, including studies of people of different races and sexual orientations, came to this conclusion: "practicing unprotected sexual intercourse with a committed relationship partner who is not tested for HIV appears to be a major and unrecognized source of HIV risk." When a relationship becomes close and committed, partners seem to believe that it is therefore safe. People whose relationships are just beginning are more cautious. Counter-intuitively, they end up better protected.

I'll end with my usual disclaimer. I'm not saying that you shouldn't get married if that's what you want to do. I'm not saying that marriage can never succeed. But I am cautioning you to beware of the marital mythology and the baseless stigmatizing of people who are single. Don't believe that singles are more self-centered than married people - they're not. Don't believe that you should be governed by other people's ideas of how you should live your sexual life (or any other aspect of your life). Live the life that feels authentic and fulfilling to you. No matter what it is, there will be challenges and rewards.

50.

What Counts as Normal?

"Different" is not the same as abnormal or unhealthy

November 7, 2011 by Bella DePaulo, Ph.D. at Psychology Today

What is the most emotionally fraught word in the psychological dictionary? I bet it is not "sex" or a less polite synonym, nor any profanity. My guess is that the word that makes us fret the most is "normal."

If you think you are different from other people in some way, and have no way to evaluate what that difference means, you probably wonder whether you are "normal." In a wonderful book with a telling title, *Sex is Not a Natural Act*, psychiatry professor and former sex columnist Leonore Tiefer spelled out five meanings of "normal." (As for the title, she's serious about that. She believes that sex is NOT a natural act.)

Five Meanings of Normal

Because Tiefer's book is about sex, I'll use that topic for the examples. The meanings of normal, though, are not specific to that topic.

1.   **Statistical.** Measure what you are interested in—frequency of sexual activity, or type of sexual behavior, for example. "Whatever behaviors are most common are normal; less frequent ones are abnormal." Tellingly, Tiefer adds, "In the United States today, 'too little sex' has joined 'too much sex' as cause for worry."

2.   **Cultural.** What is considered normal vs. deviant in your particular culture at your particular moment in time? Tiefer believes that this is the standard most of us use most of the time. What is important about it—and what Americans often do not fully appreciate—is that what is considered abnormal or deviant at one time or place is often seen as perfectly normal in another. An example from Tiefer: "In much of Oceania, mouth-to-mouth kissing was long regarded as dirty and disgusting, and yet in Europe and North America it's a major source of intimacy and arousal."

3.   **Subjective.** "I am normal and so is anyone who is the same as me." Tiefer believes that this is everyone's secret favorite definition.

4. **Idealistic.** "Perfect, an ideal to be striven for." An example: "Those who model their behavior on Christ or Gandhi...are taking an ideal for their norm, against which they measure all deviations."

5. **Clinical.** A definition based on scientific data showing that the behavior in question is linked to a disease or disability. Example: "A particular blood pressure or diet or activity is considered clinically abnormal when research shows that it is related to disease or disability."

Asexuality, Lack of Interest in Sex, and Normality

A few years ago, readers started asking me about asexuality. I did some reading and wrote this post ("Asexuals: Who are they and why are they important?"), which quickly became one of the most popular of all of my posts. Since then, when I come across a book relevant to sex, I always look for the topic of asexuality. Usually, it is just not there.

Sometimes, though, a topic that may have some relevance to asexuality (without necessarily being the same thing) appears under some other term, such as "absence of interest in sex" or "low sex drive." Here's what Leonore Tiefer has to say:

> "Who's to say, for example, that absence of interest in sex is abnormal according to the clinical definition? What sickness befalls the person who avoids sex? What disability? Clearly, such a person misses a life experience that some people value very highly and most value at least somewhat, but is avoiding sex 'unhealthy' in the same way that avoiding protein is? Avoiding sex seems more akin to avoiding travel or avoiding swimming...it's not trendy, but it's not sick, is it?"

> [To call something clinically abnormal] "I would want to see that there were negative consequences to the person's well-being other than a sense of shame or guilt from being different."

As long as people such as Leonore Tiefer continue to remind us that different is not the same as abnormal, enlightenment and consciousness-raising will have some wins, and fewer people will feel pained about their own variations from the norm, when there are no harmful consequences. One such step forward occurred just this fall, when the 40th anniversary edition of *Our Bodies, Ourselves* included "asexual" in its glossary of sexual orientations.

51.

Asexuals: Who Are They and Why Are They Important?

We have so much more to learn about asexuality

December 23, 2009 by Bella DePaulo, Ph.D. at Psychology Today

ASEXUALITY POSES A CHALLENGE TO SOME OF OUR MOST FUNDAMENTAL BELIEFS ABOUT HUMANS AND THEIR FEELINGS. YET, ON THIS TOPIC, WE ARE MOSTLY IGNORAMUSES. MANY AMERICANS REGARD THE PREVAILING ASSUMPTIONS ABOUT **SEX** AND SEXUALITY AS UNIVERSAL. THEY DON'T APPRECIATE THE WAYS THAT THESE IDEAS HAVE CHANGED OVER THE COURSE OF HISTORY. EVEN WITHIN THE SCIENTIFIC COMMUNITY, THE STUDY OF ASEXUALITY AS AN ORIENTATION IS STARKLY UNDERDEVELOPED.

Recently, I asked for suggestions for updates for the 40th anniversary edition of that classic book, Our Bodies, Ourselves. Kris suggested a new section on asexuality, and pointed readers to asexuality.org, the Asexual Visibility and Education Network. I checked it out - it is a terrific resource - and also started searching for academic papers.

The first thing I learned is that there is a startlingly small number of serious studies of asexuality. Type "asexual" into a database such as PsycInfo, and what spills out are mostly discussions of whether old people are sexual beings.

Only a few more comprehensive articles pop up. For example, a 2004 study in the JOURNAL OF SEX RESEARCH reported the results of a national sample of more than 18,000 British residents. About 1% described themselves as asexual.

For this topic, though, what should come first is some basic understanding of what the term asexual means. The best source I found on that, and the one I will refer to most often throughout the rest of this post, is a 2008 article by Kristin Scherrer published in the journal SEXUALITIES. In addition to her thoughtful conceptual analysis of asexuality, Scherrer contributes some empirical grounding. With the help of asexuality.org, she recruited 102 asexuals who were willing to answer open-ended questions about their asexuality and how that related to the rest of their lives.

Here are some of the basics of what I've learned so far from Scherrer and others. I want to note, though, that our understandings may change as research and writing on this topic grows.

What ASEXUALITY Is

On its homepage, Asexuality.org defines an asexual as "A PERSON WHO DOES NOT EXPERIENCE SEXUAL ATTRACTION." This is a definition about desire - how you feel, and not about sexual behavior - how you act.

Beyond the dimensions of feelings and behaviors is something broader - an asexual identity. There a process of self-examination involved in identifying as asexual. Importantly, though, an identity is not just personal - it is also social, cultural, and interpersonal. Asexuals who come together on asexuality.org to share experiences are building a community. They have the potential to engage in consciousness-raising and collective action, too. Health and mental health professionals, for instance, may be a little less quick to pathologize asexuality (see below) if there is a defined group of asexuals keeping the opinion leaders on their toes.

When the 102 asexuals in Scherrer's study discussed the meaning of their own asexuality, they most often pointed to desires: They said they did not experience sexual attraction or desire. One of the participants, Jenn, said this:

> "I just don't feel sexual attraction to people. I love the human form and can regard individuals as works of art and find people aesthetically pleasing, but I don't ever want to come into sexual contact with even the most beautiful of people."

Others, though, said they did feel sexual attraction but not the inclination to act on it. Sarah said this to the researcher:

> "I am sexually attracted to men but have no desire or need to engage in sexual or even non-sexual activity (cuddling, hand-holding, etc.)."

What Asexuality Is NOT

1. ASEXUALITY IS NOT THE SAME AS SEXUAL DYSFUNCTION.

If you are different from the norm, or what is perceived as the norm, you can count on the labeling police - and even some medical professionals - to tag you as dysfunctional. One of the great contributions of the web, and sites like asexuality.org, is that people can find others like them more readily than they ever could before. Comparing notes and experiences, they can find that aspects of their lives are shared, and - contrary to the conventional wisdom - are not at all undermining of their health or well-being.

Psychiatrists and psychologists sometimes see a lack of sexual desire as a symptom of an official disorder. Here, for example, is a description of Sexual Aversion Disorder: "Persistent or recurring aversion to or avoidance of sexual activity. The aversion must result in significant distress for the individual and is not better accounted for by another disorder or physical diagnosis. When presented with a sexual opportunity, the individual may experience panic attacks or extreme anxiety." The important point here is that to count as a disorder, the experience must result in "significant distress."

There is a problem in leaping from the fact of a lack of sexual desire to a label of a sexual disorder: You need to stop along the way to ask how asexuality is experienced in an individual's life. If you are okay with it, then everyone else should back off and keep their pathological labels locked in their file cabinets.

2. ASEXUALITY IS NOT THE SAME AS CELIBACY.

From asexuality.org: "Unlike celibacy, which is a choice, asexuality is a sexual orientation. Asexual people have the same emotional needs as everybody else and are just as capable of forming intimate relationships."

3. A DISINTEREST IN CUDDLING OR OTHER FORMS OF PHYSICAL AFFECTION IS NOT A NECESSARY PART OF ASEXUALITY.

Sarah (quoted above) said she had no interest in any kind of physical affection, not even hand-holding or cuddling. Others, though, do like those kinds of interactions. For instance, when asked to describe her ideal relationship, Rita said this:

> "The same as a 'normal' relationship, without the sex. We would be best friends, companions, biggest fans of each other, partners in financial, work, and social areas of our lives. I am very physical. I would like to be able to tackle my lover (as in, 'I love him', not as in 'person I am currently having sex with') to the ground, roll around until I pin him, then plant a kiss on his nose, snuggle into the crook of his arm, and talk about some random topic... without him getting an erection or entertaining hopes that this will lead to the removal of clothing or a march to the bedroom."

4. A DISINTEREST IN ROMANCE IS NOT A NECESSARY PART OF ASEXUALITY.

Rita, the asexual person quoted just above, described an ideal relationship that was in many ways a romantic one. Other asexuals are uninterested in romance. Kisha, for instance, said this in response to the question about her ideal relationship:

> "I've already got a friendship that feels a lot like my ideal relationship. We have a ton of common interests...We laugh, we think the same, we never fight or cause any burdens to each other...That's all I want, just great friendships. I don't need attraction or anything physical."

Asexuals who are romantic often identify as heterosexual, gay or lesbian, or bisexual. For those who are "aromantic," those distinctions seem irrelevant. Noting that the gender of the other person was unimportant to her, Nora said, "I am attracted to personality." Mona added, "The things I find attractive, I find attractive in both sexes."

5. A LACK OF PLEASURE FROM YOUR OWN BODY IS NOT A NECESSARY PART OF ASEXUALITY.

Some asexuals consider masturbation a sexual act and are uninterested in it. Others, such as Gloria, have a different perspective:

> "I do not have any desire to have sex with another person. I masturbate at times but I don't connect it with anything sexual. I know it sounds like a contradiction but it's just something I do every now and then."

Why Asexuality is Important

Taking asexuality seriously is a very big deal. To document a sizable number of people who do not experience sexual attraction is to challenge one of the most fundamental assumptions of contemporary society - that sexuality is pervasive, a given, an essential part of what it is to be human.

When I wrote previously about Sex and the Single Person, I emphasized how important it is to take the long view of sex and sexuality and appreciate how our assumptions have changed over the course of history. In contemporary Western societies, sexual experiences (and lots of them) are believed to be a defining feature of the good life. That's great for people who love having sex and can readily find partners. Others, though, such as the involuntarily celibate, or the happily asexual, are likely to feel marginalized.

52.

Getting Married and Getting Sex (or Not)

Here's what the research on marital status and sex really does show

February 6, 2010 by Bella DePaulo, Ph.D. at Psychology Today

In a recent post, I argued that a book called THE CASE FOR *Marriage* has perpetrated many of the false claims about the benefits of getting married. It does so by supposedly drawing from the professional research literature. I looked at the claims in the book, and compared them to the published version of the research they cite. The results are not pretty. Here's an example, from a section of Singled Out: How Singles Are Stereotyped, Stigmatized, and Ignored, and Still Live Happily Ever After (pp. 52-55).

EXCERPT FROM Singled Out:

Getting Married and Getting Sex

I bet you can anticipate the bottom line of Waite and Gallagher's chapter on sex. Married couples have more sex and better sex.

There is only one problem with that conclusion: It is not exactly true. Married people do not have the most sex - cohabiting people do.

If I were in Waite and Gallagher's place and wanted to defend married people's second place finish in the sexual frequency sweepstakes, I'd say that raw frequency means nothing apart from desired frequency. So what if co-habitors are having the most sex if one partner wants even more and the other wishes there were a whole lot less? Maybe married people are more likely to get the amount of sex that they want.

Waite and Gallagher try to shrug off the more active sex lives of co-habitors in a different way. Co-habiting relationships, they say, are more likely than marriages to be "built around sex." In Waite and Gallagher's view, married people who are not having sex still consider themselves to be married, but if co-habiting people are not having sex, then they just consider themselves to be roommates.

Does that sound unconvincing? That's OK. Waite and Gallagher are ready with another way to diminish the people who are having more sex than married people: "They don't seem to enjoy it quite as much." In support of their conclusion that married people have more extremely satisfying sex than other people do, Waite and Gallagher cite a lot of percentages. Those numbers are listed in the first column of data in the table below. In the adjacent column are actual numbers from the original source, The National Sex Survey.

What Percentage of People are Extremely Emotionally Satisfied with their Sex Lives?

Using Waite and Gallagher's Categories

WAITE AND GALLAGHER'S NUMBERS (WG)
Actual Numbers from the National Sex Survey (Actual)

MEN

Married men:	**48 (WG)**, **48.9 (Actual)**
Co-habiting men:	**37 (WG)**, **35.2** for single co-habitors,
	52.6 for div/sep co-habitors (**Actual**)

WOMEN

Married women:	**42 (WG)**, **42.1 (Actual)**
Single women with sexual partner:	**31 (WG) 31.4** for not co-habiting,
	44.1 for co-habiting (**Actual**)
Divorced with sexual partner:	**27 (WG)**, **27.4** for not co-habiting
	36.5 for co-habiting (**Actual**)

Waite and Gallagher were reasonably accurate when they described the satisfaction of married people. When you compare the percentages they report for the married men and married women to the actual percentages from the National Sex Survey, the two sets are similar. But Waite and Gallagher really did a number on everyone else.

Take, for example, this claim: "For men, having a wife beats shacking up by a wide margin: 48 percent of husbands say sex with their partner is extremely satisfying emotionally, compared to just 37 percent of cohabiting men." Now look at the second row of numbers in the table (the one corresponding to the co-habiting men). Yes, 37 percent is close enough to the actual number of single co-habiting men who describe their sex as extremely emotionally satisfying. But Waite and Gallagher do not happen to mention that for divorced men who are co-habiting, the number is 52.6 percent. That amounts to more sexually satisfied co-habiting divorced men than married men. And that is not the case that Waite and Gallagher are trying to make.

To make the married women look good, they take a different tack. They compare the sexual satisfaction of married women to that of the single and divorced women who are not co-habiting. That's convenient, because, as you can see from the table, it is the co-habiting women who usually report the more satisfying sex lives.

The National Sex Survey was full of information about rates of sexual problems. Waite and Gallagher do not have much to say on that topic. Here's some of what they skipped over. With regard to some of the problems men might have, such as an inability to maintain an erection, climaxing too early, or experiencing pain during sex, currently married men have nothing over men who have always been single. When the two groups differ on those measures, it is the married men who are more likely to be having difficulties. Men who have always been single also report fewer sexual problems than divorced men.

Among the women, the group most likely to be problem-free is not the currently married women. Rather, it is the widowed women who are less likely than all of the others (married, divorced, separated, or always single) to complain that they do not find sex pleasurable, that they cannot reach orgasm or they reach it too early, or that they experience anxiety or pain during sex.

Waite and Gallagher wrap up their chapter on the sexual advantages of marriage by describing the results of one last survey. This one, sponsored by the Family Research Council, described all the people who could lay claim to the most satisfying sex. Married people, of course, top the list, but some married people are even better off sexually than others. Among them are: those who attend church weekly, who believe that out-of-wedlock sex is wrong, who have three or more children, who live in one-earner households, and "who see sex as a sacred union, exclusive to marriage." There is an endnote corresponding to the description of these results. It says that the Family Research Council "is an activist not a scholarly organization." Indeed. According to their website, the Council "champions marriage and family as the foundation of civilization, the seedbed of virtue, and the wellspring of society." Also, it "promotes the Judeo-Christian worldview as the basis for a just, free, and stable society."

In all of the research I described in this section, people were surveyed about their sexual behavior at one point in time. As always, that means that any differences between people may have had nothing whatsoever to do with getting married. The sexual behavior of the married people, for example, may have been the same even before they married. So far as I know, there are no published studies of sex in which the same people are studied over time, as their marital status changes or remains the same.

END OF EXCERPT

53.

Are Monogamous Relationships Really Better?

Science scrutinizes monogamy

December 20, 2012 by Bella DePaulo, Ph.D. in Psychology Today

In one way, the answer to the question in the title of this article, "Are monogamous relationships really better," is obvious. If the criterion is, do people THINK they are better, then the answer is an overwhelming yes.

Being monogamous has a similar ideological sheen to getting married – it is something that we think we are SUPPOSED to do. Ask people why everyone should be monogamous/get married, and they will easily generate reasons for why it is better to do so than to be non-monogamous/ stay single.

I have done lots of studies of stereotypes of single people. Terri Conley and her colleagues have been studying stereotypes of people who have what they call "consensually non-mongamous" (**CNM**) relationships. We have each gone on to answer the next question: Are the stereotypes true, or are they mostly myths and prejudices?

I.   First, some definitions.

Conley likes the CDC definition of **monogamy**: "mutual monogamy means that you agree to be sexually active with just one person, and that person has agreed to be sexually active only with you."

Consensually non-monogamous relationships (CNM) are "relationships in which both partners have openly agreed that they and/or their partners will have other sexual or romantic partners."

Polyamory involves "having consensual loving and romantic relationships with more than one partner." That's different from **swinging** or **open relationships**, in which the relationships may be just sexual and not necessarily loving or romantic.

II.   My dog in this fight.

My dog is the one that isn't keeping everyone awake and annoyed with its barking. I think contemporary American society has gotten carried away with its insistence that there is a right way to engage in sex (have lots of it, with just one person – or just one at a time). I think we should recognize that all sorts of approaches to sex (including asexuality and CNM) can be just fine for some people, and we should not keep trying to make everyone act and feel the same way. (This is not an endorsement of hurtful sex, of course.)

My other dog is science. If we (royal we) are going to proclaim that one kind of sex is best, then my answer to that is: Show me the data.

III.   The research.

There is not all that much research on CNM. As Conley points out, scientists seem so sure that monogamy is best that they have not bothered to do all that much research on the matter. Conley and her colleagues now have an ongoing program of research, and they have also reviewed research from other labs. (Reference is at the end.)

Does monogamy provide "a life full of safe and excellent sex"?

That's one of the assumptions about monogamy – that it brings all sorts of sexual benefits. But research shows that "sexual frequency, on average, decreases over the course of a (presumed monogamous) romantic relationship." There is also evidence to suggest that sexual desire decreases over the course of a long-term romantic relationship.

As for how safe the sex is in monogamous vs. CNM relationships, the assumption is that monogamous sex is safer. The research disagrees. What seems to happen is that people assume there is more safety in their supposedly monogamous relationships than there is in fact. As Conley put it, "couples put condoms away, typically within the first couple months of dating, and switch to other forms of birth control when they feel comfortable with one another, rather than after objective testing for STIs." (STIs are sexually transmitted infections.) In long-term relationships, including many marriages, partners often do not take into account the very real possibility of infidelity.

Here are more specifics of the research findings. (I'm taking a paragraph from the article and turning the sentences into bullet points, for ease of reading.)

- "Sexually unfaithful individuals were less likely to use barriers during their extradyadic encounter, less likely to tell their partner about the encounter, and less likely to be tested for STIs than individuals in CNM relationships."

- "Sexually unfaithful individuals were less likely to use barrier methods in their primary relationship than CNM individuals."

- "People in ostensibly monogamous relationships were also more likely to make condom use mistakes."

- "Individuals often use condoms or other barrier methods more frequently with casual partners than with 'regular' partners."

Reference:

Conley, T. D., Ziegler, A., Moors, A. C., Matsick, J. L., & Valentine, B. (2012). A critical examination of popular assumptions about the benefits and outcomes of monogamous relationships. ***Personality*** AND SOCIAL PSYCHOLOGY REVIEW.

VIII.

Are We Missing Out by Being Single – Or Are They?

54.

23 Ways Single People Are Better: The Scientific Evidence

A lot of research shows that single life is superior

May 4, 2014 by Bella DePaulo, Ph.D. at Psychology Today

A few months ago, a reporter asked me if I kept a list of scientifically-documented ways in which it is better to be single than married. I could not believe that my answer was no. I have been so busy being defensive—arguing again and again that no, getting married will not make you happier and it will not make you healthier and it will not make you live longer and it will not doom your kids and it will not make your social networks blossom—that it rarely occurred to me that I should be systematically making the more pro-active case. There are ways, grounded in research, that single people do better than married people.

In response to the reporter's question, I told her what I could think of offhand, and she wrote this story, which had been nicely timed for Valentine's Day. (The reporter, by the way, was Lauren F. Friedman, who used to be an editor here at PSYCHOLOGY TODAY.) Ever since, I have been working on my own list. It is not yet complete (and will continue to be a work in progress), so please do let me know what I've missed.

[My usual caveat: Some studies compare people of different marital or relationship statuses at just one point in time. As I have often explained, the results of such studies are open to different interpretations. True experiments are impossible, since people can't be randomly assigned to get married or stay single, but longitudinal studies, in which the same people are followed over time, are better than the studies comparing people at just one point in time.]

Single People are Healthier

#1 People who have always been single exercise more than married people do. Divorced people exercise more than married people, too, but not as much as the people who have always been single.

#2 Among wounded warriors, the ones who have always been single are the most resilient. The RAND Corporation has been studying members of the military who have been wounded since 9/11. Compared to those who were married or divorced, the warriors who had always been single were least likely to have symptoms suggesting PTSD, most successful at bouncing back from injury or illness or hardship, least likely to be depressed, least likely to be obese, and least likely to have emotional or physical health problems that interfered with their work or other regular activities.

#3 Women who get married get fatter. CDC data suggests that the same may be true for men (pp. 43-46 of Singled Out), though their study was based on just one point in time.

#4 Always-single men are less likely than men of any other marital status to experience heart disease. Results are from an 8-year study of heart disease in mid-life, based on a representative sample of Americans. The always-single women looked good, too, but the results were particularly striking for the men.

#5 Women who have always been single have better overall health than currently married women. They also have fewer days in bed because of disabilities and fewer doctors' visits. Results were from the National Health Interview Study (of women only).

#6 Women who have always been single are healthier than men who are currently married. That's from the most recent year analyzed of a study that has been ongoing for decades.

#7 All those ED ads? They're for you, married men. From p. 54 of Singled Out: "With regard to some of the problems men might have, such as an inability to maintain an erection, climaxing too early, or experiencing pain during sex, currently married men have nothing over men who have always been single. When the two groups differ on those measures, it is the married men who are more likely to be having difficulties." (Also check out: "Getting married and getting sex (or not)" and "Sex and the single person.")

Single People Are Keeping Friends, Siblings, Parents, and Communities Together

#8 People who get married become less connected to their friends and their parents than they were when they were single. That's not just a newlywed effect – it continues for as many years into the marriage as researchers have studied.

#9 People who have always been single are more attentive to friends, family, and neighbors than people who are married. This can't be explained away by time spent on kids. Among those who have young kids and those who have no kids, the marrieds are again less attentive to their friends and parents.

#10 Single people are more likely than married ones to keep siblings together in their adult lives. Follow people over time, and the ones who get married have less contact with their siblings than they did when they were single. If they get divorced, though, they will start connecting with their siblings more than they did when they were married.

#11 Single people have a more diverse set of confidants than married people do. Both single and married people name kin as important people in their lives, but single people are more likely to also name people who are not kin.

#12 Single people are more likely to volunteer for civic organizations than married people are. That's from Eric Klinenberg's *Going Solo*.

Single People Are Better with Money than Married People Are

#13 Single people have less debt than married people do, and that's true even when the married people do not have kids.

In the Workplace, Single People Are More Likely than Married People to Care About More than Just Money

#14 Single people are less materialistic than married people are.

#15 Single people are more likely to value meaningful work.

#16 In a study of men only, men who got married spent less time in work-related pursuits that did not benefit just them (such as professional societies, unions, and farm organizations) than they did when they were single. They don't spend any more time in political groups, service clubs, or fraternal organizations than they did when they were single.

Single People Get More Emotional Rewards from Solitude and Self-Sufficiency and Maybe from Themselves

#17 Solitude brings many rewards to those who value it. People who are single—especially those who are single at heart, seem especially likely to value solitude and benefit from it. (See also, 6 psychological insights about solitude and 20 varieties of solitude.)

#18 People vary in how self-sufficient they are, but everyone needs some self-sufficiency at least some of the time. For people who have always been single, their self-sufficiency seems to protect them from bad feelings: The more self-sufficient they are, the less likely they are to experience negative emotions. For married people, the reverse is true: The more self-sufficient they are, the more likely they are to experience negative emotions.

#19 It is even possible that singles are better at being their own sources of comfort and security, though so far, the relevant data are just suggestive.

Single People Are More Generous and Helpful

#20 Married people exchange much <u>LESS</u> help with their parents and parents-in-law combined than single people do with just their parents. It is the single people who are there for mom and dad.

#21 A study that included only men found that men who got married were less generous to their friends than they were when they were single. They were not any more generous with their relatives. This is especially noteworthy because single men are paid less than married men, even when they are equally accomplished.

#22 Single people are more likely than married people to have regularly looked after someone who was sick or disabled or elderly, for at least three months.

Bottom Line: Resilience

#23 My bottom line? I think single people are more resilient than everyone else. But as we social scientists are taught to say in our scholarly publications, more research is needed.

55.

What You Miss by Doing What Everyone Else Does

A new take on "you don't know what you're missing"

October 8, 2011 by Bella DePaulo, Ph.D. at Psychology Today

An unlikely figure graced the cover of a recent issue of HOLLYWOOD REPORTER. Rachel Maddow, the highly successful host of The Rachel Maddow Show on MSNBC, is not exactly your standard-issue female anchor with blond hair, predictable prettiness, short skirts, and high heels. Instead, she is tall, with short dark hair and wears simple blazers. She is also, as the **HOLLYWOOD REPORTER** notes, "the first openly gay person to host a primetime news program."

Rachel lives with her partner Susan and is not shy about mentioning Susan on her show. In a publication with a name like **THE HOLLYWOOD REPORTER**, you know what question she is going to get asked—when are you two getting married?

Rachel uses her platform to push relentlessly for rights for the LGBT community. With regard to Don't Ask, Don't Tell, for instance, she just never gave up. But when she gets asked The Question, here's what she says, **"WE KNOW A LOT OF PEOPLE WHO HAVE GOTTEN MARRIED BUT I DON'T THINK WE FEEL ANY URGENCY ABOUT IT."**

The article continues:

> **LATER SHE ADMITS THAT SHE'S ACTUALLY AMBIVALENT ABOUT THE CULTURAL IMPACT OF GAY MARRIAGE.**
>
> **"I FEEL THAT GAY PEOPLE NOT BEING ABLE TO GET MARRIED FOR GENERATIONS, FOREVER, MEANT THAT WE CAME UP WITH ALTERNATIVE WAYS OF RECOGNIZING RELATIONSHIPS," SHE EXPLAINS. "AND I WORRY THAT IF EVERYBODY HAS ACCESS TO THE SAME INSTITUTIONS THAT WE LOSE THE CREATIVITY OF SUBCULTURES HAVING TO MAKE IT ON THEIR OWN. AND I LIKE GAY CULTURE."**

As single people, we are often lectured on what we are supposedly missing by not being married (and if we are not parents, by not having children). What I love about Rachel Maddow's observations is that they raise the flip side of that perspective, a side that is so very rarely addressed - what married people miss by not being single. Or, more broadly, what people miss when they just go ahead and do what everyone else does.

If you are single—especially if you are living your single life fully, joyfully, and without apology, rather than simply looking to become unsingle—think of all that you have in your life that you may have missed out on (or marginalized) if you were married in the conventional sense. If you married and practiced intensive coupling, whereby you and your spouse aspire to be everything to each other, it is true that you would have each other (well, for as long as your union lasts), but what would you not have?

For example:

- Would you have the same personal community that you have now? Perhaps you have friends, relatives, neighbors, mentors, coworkers and other people who are important to you, and to whom you devote as much or as little time and attention as you like. You have friends, and you can, if you want to, spend more time with them because you do NOT have friends-in-law. Friends-in-law are those people who come attached to the person you really do like, when that person is coupled and does not like to venture out without the other half.

- Would you have the same potential to indulge in sweet solitude, spending time on your own when that is what you prefer?

- Would you have a place of your own, or a part of a place that is organized and adorned in the way that best suits you, including the option of not organizing it or not adorning it at all?

- Would you have the job you wanted most (of those that you could obtain) or would you have the job that you would have to settle for in order to accommodate a spouse's wishes?

- Would you have pursued your passions in the ways you do now?

- Would you be able to manage your time and your interests in the way you do now?

- Would you be living where you most want to live (within your resources)?

56.

What We Miss by Thinking the Same Way as Everyone Else

Single people ask better questions

November 21, 2011 by Bella DePaulo, Ph.D at PsychCentral

For a long time, I didn't really understand why diversity was important in any deep sense. Sure, I believe in equal opportunity as a basic tenet of fairness in America, and that was reason enough to want to see all different kinds of people in classrooms, neighborhoods, and boardrooms. What I did not get was how people who are not like everyone else can see things in profoundly different ways.

They ask different questions, offer fresh interpretations, and notice what's missing or misleading in the conventional wisdom, in the popular media, and even in academic writings.

If you are someone who does not fit into the standard American box – because of your race or sexual orientation or religion or any other important characteristic – then you already know what I'm talking about. I didn't learn these things until I started studying the science of relationships from the perspective of someone who is single at heart.

When I say that I am single at heart, I mean that single is who I really am. I'm not pining for a partner. I have been single my entire life and I plan to stay that way. I love my single life (except for all of the stereotyping and discrimination that I call SINGLISM). Even if you are not as committed to single life as I am, but simply want to live your single years as fully and joyfully as possible, you are more likely to bring new ways of thinking to psychological research than people who care more about the coupled (romantic) relationship than any other.

Here are some examples.

Generating Plausible Explanations that No One Else Thought of

A scholar describing the findings of her research on siblings said this:

"WHERE ONE SIBLING IS SINGLE, THERE TENDS TO BE MORE CONTACT THAN BETWEEN MARRIED PEOPLE."

Her explanation is this:

"THE SIBLING RELATIONSHIP MAY BE SEEN BY ADULTS AS COMPENSATORY, IN THE SENSE THAT THERE IS MORE CONTACT BETWEEN SIBLINGS WHEN ONE OF THEM DOES NOT HAVE AN INTIMATE PARTNER."

Before you read the next sentence, can you generate your own interpretation of the findings that is different from the one you just read? The author is saying that singles pay more attention to siblings than married people do because they are "compensating" for not having a spouse. What do you think?

How about this:

- Single people are better at maintaining the relationships they care about. OR

- Single people prefer to have a diversified relationship portfolio, maintaining contact with different kinds of people such as siblings, friends, and neighbors, rather than focusing primarily on just one other person (the spouse or romantic partner).

Asking Questions that are Farther-Reaching

An important review article published in a prestigious psychology journal set out to answer this question:

WHAT ARE THE IMPLICATIONS OF MULTIPLE ROLES (E.G., WORKER, HOUSEKEEPER, CAREGIVER) FOR THE WELL-BEING OF HUSBANDS AND WIVES AND FOR THEIR RELATIONSHIP?

That's a question worth addressing. Can you take the same basic issue (the implications of multiple roles for well-being) and pose a question that is based on a bigger, broader point of view?

How about this:

- What are the implications of having had multiple roles (compared to just one role) for well-being AFTER a marriage ends? OR

- What are the implications of multiple roles for all people (singles included) across the lifespan?

Recognizing When Intentions to be Inclusive Are Actually Exclusive

See if you can tell what is wrong with these two statements:

- In its recruiting materials, an organization makes this claim: HERE AT COMPANY PRIMO, WE CARE ABOUT WORK-FAMILY BALANCE.

- Boastful claim by a politician: I CARE ABOUT WORKING FAMILIES.

Company Primo wants its prospective employees to know that it cares about more than just their work life. Such a company probably also construes "family" in the narrow sense of the nuclear family that adults "create." More than 40% of all workers are single. Many of them do not have children. The "work-family balance" promise is unlikely to speak to their wishes to live full lives outside of the workplace, or to care for people who may be especially important to them, such as siblings or close friends.

The politician probably intends to convey the message that she or he does not just care about the elites. The working class is important, too. Then why not express a concern for all workers? "Working families" is an odd concept. Employers do not hire families, they hire individual workers. And anyway, 2-year olds are not all that great at driving trucks or designing websites.

57.

Two Scholars Ask: What if Marriage Is Bad for Us?

What if everything you think you know about marriage is wrong?

December 12, 2009 by Bella DePaulo, Ph.D. at Psychology Today

People who dislike my writings are fond of calling me anti-marriage, but that's not quite accurate. What I really think is that marriage is not for everyone, and that people who want to stay single should not be targeted with singlism because of it. People who marry should refrain from becoming matrimaniacs, as should the rest of the society. I believe, based on a close reading of original scientific sources, that most of the demeaning claims about single people are grossly exaggerated or just plain wrong. I also question the status of marriage as a criterion of eligibility for such basic human dignities as access to health care (as when marrieds can access health insurance through a spouse's plan but singles have no comparable option) or to a secure retirement (as when a widow can access their deceased spouse's Social Security benefits but singles can neither receive benefits from, say, a close friend or sibling, nor can they bequeath their benefits to any such peers).

Earlier this fall, two scholars posed a starker question than my own: "What if marriage is bad for us?" The essay by Middlebury College sociologists Laurie Essig and Lynn Owens was originally published in the CHRONICLE OF HIGHER EDUCATION and later reprinted elsewhere.

The scholars begin by reviewing the usual claims about all the ways in which marriage is supposed to be good for us. They also take us through some of the segments of society, from progressive advocacy groups to conservative (and not-at-all-conservative) political leaders who have tried so hard to advance those beliefs.

Then they pivot and take on the claims, one after another. For example:

1. In response to the pronouncement that "marriage makes you healthy," they note (as I often have) that "married and never-married Americans are similar; it's the divorced who seem to suffer." They then dare to add this: "The lesson might be to never divorce, but an even more obvious lesson to be drawn from the research might be to never marry."

2. About the myth that single people are isolated and alone, the authors point to research showing that actually, married couples are more often isolated. They note that "we are instructed by movies, pop songs, state policy, and sociology to get married because 'love is all you need.' But actually we humans need more."

3. Does marriage make you rich? Not necessarily. And, "even when marriage does produce wealth, divorce often destroys it."

4. Surely we can all agree that marriage is traditional? No, even that well-worn assumption does not pass muster. As the authors (and others) have noted, "marriage has changed over time and exists differently in different cultures." But even if mate choices were once based on considerations such as who had the best fields and who would keep the goods in the right lineages, aren't contemporary marriages based on love? Here, Essig and Owens remind us of Laura Kipnis's decidedly unromantic notion of marriage as a "'domestic gulag,' a forced-labor camp where the inmates have to spend all of their time outside of work working on their marriage."

A few other points worth pondering:

5. Noting that the rate of marriage has dropped, and that the levels of happiness among those who do marry have also slumped, the authors muse: "Maybe it's the decline in happiness that has caused an increasing number of Americans to say 'I don't,' despite Hollywood's presenting us with happy ending after happy ending and a government bent on distributing civil rights on the basis of marital status. Apparently no amount of propaganda or coercion can force humans to participate in a family form so out of sync with what we actually need."

6. Finally, in response to those who would suggest that loneliness is the only alternative to a lifelong marriage, Essig and Owens have this to say: "Instead of 'blaming the victims' for failing to adopt the formative lifestyles of the white and middle class, we should consider that those avoiding marriage might know exactly what they are doing. Marriage is not necessarily good for all of us, and it might even be bad for most of us. When there is broad, seemingly unanimous support for an institution, and when the institution is propped up by such disparate ideas as love, civil rights, and wealth creation, we should wonder why so many different players seem to agree so strongly. Perhaps it's because they are supporting not just marriage but also the status quo."

58.

Top 8 Reasons Not to Marry

Values, identity, and justice motivate the not-married life

November 19, 2013 by Bella DePaulo, Ph.D. at Psychology Today

Long-time readers know how much I detest those "why you are single" stories that point fingers at the supposed flaws of people who are not married. It is time to flip the script, and list some of the most important, non-singlist reasons for not marrying.

I started thinking about this most recently when the NEW YORK TIMES published the story, "Gay couples, choosing to say 'I don't.'" Many of the reasons gay couples offered for not marrying are also embraced by heterosexual couples (and singles) who are just not getting swept up in the relentless matrimania.

Here's my list of **Top 8 Reasons Not to Marry**, which includes some of the reasons noted in the TIMES as well as a few of my own.

#1 Number one on my list of reasons for why people do not marry is that they are single-at-heart. Living single is how they live their most meaningful and fulfilling lives.

#2 Other single people are open to marrying but they won't marry just for the sake of marrying. They have standards. That doesn't make them "too picky;" it makes them wise.

The next two reasons are based on arguments about injustice:

#3 The injustice argument that is most familiar and has been around the longest: Marriage is not so great for women. Historically, women have been oppressed in marriage. Even in contemporary marriages, women still generally do more of the housework and the child care (when there are children) than men do.

#4 The injustice argument that still has not gotten the attention it deserves: Marriage is unfair to single people. From the matrimania that confers unearned status to the laws that grant undeserved benefits, protections, and privileges, marriage creates a caste system. No one should be proud of that.

Other reasons not to marry follow from values and aspirations; for people who endorse such reasons, the values of marriage seem too small or too constraining.

#5 Marriage can impose an unwelcome self-definition. The TIMES story offered several examples of this perspective. One came from LGBT activist Paula Ettelbrick who once said, "I do not want to be known as 'Mrs. Attached-to-Somebody-Else.'" Catharine Stimpson, previously a dean at NYU, told the TIMES that getting married would undermine her "edgy nonconformist streak." John D'Emilio, author of *Intimate Matters: A History of Sexuality in America* (among other important works), believes that same-sex marriage is elitist.

#6 The marriage mentality overvalues one particular relationship and undervalues a wide range of other relationships, some of which are more egalitarian. The overvaluing is practiced by married people who look to their spouse to be their Sex and Everything Else Partner (or Seepie, as I called it in *Singled Out*). The undervaluing happens when everyone else other than the spouse gets back-burnered, including long-time friends.

#7 Another reason is a set of practical concerns: People simply do not want the financial or legal entanglements that marriage entails.

#8 Finally, there's the data-based argument: Marriage has failed to pass the empirical test; too many marriages end in divorce. Less widely recognized is that the many purported benefits of marrying, from greater happiness to better health, are greatly exaggerated or just not there (as I argued in *Singled Out* and have continued to show with my critiques of each new study purporting to demonstrate such benefits).

59.

Keeping Marriage Alive with Affairs, Asexuality, Polyamory, and Living Apart

Rather than stretching marriage beyond recognition, why not live single?

June 2, 2011 by Bella DePaulo, Ph.D. at Psychology Today

Pamela Haag's provocative new book is MARRIAGE CONFIDENTIAL: THE POST-ROMANTIC AGE OF WORKHORSE WIVES, ROYAL CHILDREN, UNDERSEXED SPOUSES, AND REBEL COUPLES WHO ARE REWRITING THE RULES. The 21st century, she argues, is a post-romantic age of melancholy marriages. The couples are not acutely stressed nor entangled in constant conflict - they are just melancholy. They signed up for the marriage pact and lost a vital part of themselves in the process.

Here, I will go through a few of the problems Haag describes as plaguing contemporary marriages, and tell you about some of the solutions she learned about in her research and interviews. Remember, her goal is not to generate alternatives to marriage but alternatives WITHIN marriage that have the potential to keep the marriages together. To longtime readers of Living Single, I bet you will anticipate the conclusion I am leading up to before you get to the end of this post.

1.   **The problem of the insularity of many modern marriages** (the "Marriage as a Bomb Shelter" issue). From Haag:

> "Marriage is touted as the 'building block' of civilization. But what civilization, if all we do is tend to our own, important though that is? We'll end up with a million building blocks and no foundation."

Pamela Haag has discovered that married couples are already exploring options to living in their single-family moat-encircled private castles. They range from co-housing to living in homes with separate master bedrooms to continuing to cohabit even after divorcing to living in separate homes while staying married.

2.   **"The underwhelming crisis of infidelity**." Yes, that's what Pamela Haag has concluded about the supposed crisis of extramarital affairs - it is underwhelming. In theory, we abhor affairs - and in fact, some truly are extraordinarily cruel and hurtful. But more often than we might guess, Haag

finds, spouses react with little more than a shrug. She offers some thoughts about what this is about:

> "...perhaps infidelity is about what it appears to be able: sexual ennui if not desperation in an otherwise not-bad marriage, and/or lust....Perhaps it's about wanting to get back the complexity, depth, and richness of your character again, but within the boundaries of a marriage that otherwise 'works.'"

So how do today's couples deal with affairs without divorcing? Haag founds lots of arrangements and understandings. Some maintain that 'everyone gets at least one free pass.' Others have 'only when traveling' or 'only 50 miles away' rules. There are "don't ask, don't tell couples," tell only so much couples, and tell-all couples. One wife told Haag that when she discovered that her husband was a philanderer, she "banished him temporarily to a nearby apartment, but had him come back every morning to get the children off to school and pack their lunches, and then return in the evening to cook their dinner."

3.   **The challenge of the married** asexual. Pamela Haag realizes that a sexless marriage is not the same thing as a marriage that includes an asexual. Referring to the Asexual Visibility and Education Network (AVEN), she describes married asexuals as those who

> "reject the prioritizing of monogamous sexual love over friendship. Asexual marriage doesn't mean not being intimate, or even not having sex; it means not wanting to have sex, and coveting an ideal of platonic intimacy."

What's a married couple to do if they want to stay married but only one of the two people is asexual and the other really, really likes and wants sex? Haag describes one couple who tried compromising on sex once a week. When that didn't work, the asexual wife persuaded her husband that he should just go ahead and have his affairs, and she would help him pick out his girlfriends. He, of course, thought he was being set up. He wasn't. As the wife explained:

> "Say you like Ping-Pong. I hate Ping-Pong, you love Ping-Pong, so go find someone who will play with you and have a good time doing it."

Post-romantic, indeed.

4.   **The couple who wants intimacy from more than one person**. Enter polyamory. There are different meanings of the term but Pamela Haag uses it to refer to the new open marriage, or 'ethical nonmonogamy.' The ethical part

is the "scrupulous standard of telling the truth." Partners are honest with each other about what they are doing, and they engage only with people who are honest with their partners. This version of polyamory is not just about sex - "the intimacies are real but circumscribed."

5.   **The problem of married couples begrudging one another the time they spend with friends or anything they do for fun without their spouse along for the ride**. Haag offers the analogy of what she calls the desiccated AMERICAN BEAUTY marriage:

> "It offers the husband, played by Kevin Spacey, two roles: to live either as a sexless, soul-crushingly dutiful and henpecked husband, or as a pot-smoking, self-absorbed adolescent who lusts after the high school cheerleader. There is no authentic nonparental role for him in between, no option of being a multifaceted adult."

Among the possible lifelines Haag tosses to those trapped in AMERICAN BEAUTY marriages is this one: the marriage sabbatical. Maybe the couples just need some 'growth time' apart.

I wanted to end with the notion of the marriage sabbatical because that's how I ended Singled Out. Quoting an author who had described what she loved about having time to herself and a space that was only her own, I said this:

> "Jarvis was married but craved a sabbatical from her marriage. She wanted long stretches of solitude, where she could bask, uninterrupted, in her thoughts and in her work, in her own special place. What she really wanted - at least for a while - was to be single."

So have you anticipated my conclusion - why it is that I think this book, which is all about marriage, actually furthers the cause of single people?

Consider again what Pamela Haag sees as UNNECESSARY to marriage:

a.   Children

b.   Living together

c.   Sex

d.   Having sex only with each other

e.   Having intimacy only with each other

f.   Spending all of your time - including even stretches of time that last for months or longer - with each other. (You can instead take a 'marriage sabbatical' and spend as much time on your own or with friends or anyone else, doing whatever you want, for as long as the sabbatical lasts.)

I see all this as spelling out not (just) an alternative within marriage, but an alternative TO marriage. This is single life. If you can choose a combination of these options and still call what you have a marriage, why bother? (Except, of course, to run away with all the federally-bestowed loot, and the prestige of having membership in the Married Couples Club.)

Maybe Pamela Haag would say that marriage is different because you value that lasting bond with your spouse. But many single people value and cherish deep and enduring bonds with friends, siblings, and other relatives. And since sex and living together are optional, and having very close relationships with more than one person is permissible, how is this not a description of a fulfilling single life?

To me, what Haag is describing is the best version of friendship. You can have a friend you have known for a long time and with whom you have shared everyday experiences and deep intimacies. You can have more than one such friend and (in theory) the various friends don't get to feel too possessive about that. You and your friend(s) can have different sexual preferences, including not much interest in sex at all. Your friend might have multiple sexual partners and you figure, "well, if she likes Ping Pong, she should go find some people to play with and have a good time." Even if you don't totally approve, you might try to be supportive or understanding because you care about your friend's happiness.

There are two other points from Marriage Confidential that I see as very pertinent to single life, even though Pamela Haag doesn't frame them that way.

Here's the first, in Haag's words:

> "I think of Nicole's husband and other serial monogamists who divorce their wives because they're 'in love' with a mistress. What if they had an alternative to this romantic narrative? What if they had a narrative that there are varieties of attachment, passion, and love in which passion isn't certification of 'true love'? I suspect that we end up feeling, assuming, and thinking what our prevailing stories and metaphors of marriage condition us to feel, assume, and think."

The key point is about the power of the prevailing narrative. The conventional wisdom about single people and single life is the series of degrading myths that I write about so often. Part of the power of the myths is in their prevalence and their taken-for-grantedness. One of the preeminent goals of much of my writing is to describe a new narrative about single life - one that is more accurate, because it is grounded in research rather than singlism and guesswork.

The second and last excerpt of Haag's that I want to critique is this one:

> "Betty Friedan had to expose and second-wave feminism had to remedy basic legal, economic, educational, social, and cultural inequalities that made marriage all but imperative for all women. Today we have a different, secret, and often internal struggle, to make good on the promises of our own liberation....we have unprecedented latitude to do marriage differently."

True, it is important to broaden the way we do marriage. But even more fundamental is the achievement of genuine freedom in the ways we organize our lives so that living single is a real and respected and viable life path. If our only option is to improve on marriage, then marriage is still the imperative that it was in Friedan's day.

Conclusion: Why Marriage Confidential is Good for Singles

Sometimes people ask me how my notion of single at heart differs from Sasha Cagen's quirkyalone. As I explained before, quirkyalones proclaim:

> "We are people who are happily single, with friends and passions and full lives, BUT we are also romantics. We love those silly love songs, even as we recognize their silliness. Once we find that one perfect person, 'oooh la la.'

> "The qualifier - we're happily single BUT we'd love to be coupled with the perfect person - made all the difference. Quirkyalones are not threatening to people who are coupled at heart."

Once Cagen had popularized quirkyalone, single-at-heart was less of a shock and a stretch. It became understandable (at least to some) in a way that it wasn't before.

Let's say that Pamela Haag can persuade a matrimanical society that, in the service of staving off divorce, it may actually be a good thing to condone couples who have separate living quarters or no sex or extra sex or extra intimacy. The path to accepting, respecting, and maybe even celebrating single life would then be shorter.

60.

How Many Married People Wish They Were Single?

The perils of asking only one kind of question

October 13, 2013 by Bella DePaulo, Ph.D. at Psychology Today

When I was in Finland, I met a Dutch journalist who came to the conference on living alone. Maartje Duin works for VPRO Radio, the national Dutch public broadcasting company. When I got back, I found this question (below) from her. She said it was okay to answer it on this blog and mention her by name.

One more question I didn't have time to ask you on the morning you left. I reread your blog about the amount of people who choose to be single. You refer to the 25% of people in the Pew Research Report who say they don't want to be married. That's 16% of the cohabiting couples, 12% of the singles and 46% of the divorced/widowed. But they didn't ask people if they wanted to cohabit. For the 16% of cohabiting who don't want to marry, we can assume they are fine with cohabiting. For the 12% singles and 46% divorced/widowed we don't know if they want to cohabit (but as it becomes more and more popular, we can assume the numbers are not all that low). Unless they killed their husbands or wives, widow(er)s can hardly be called singles by choice, so we take those out of the equation. So based on these results I'm not sure if 25% wants to be single. Can you convince me?

Oh Bella, one more thing: I should, of course, include people who don't want to marry nor cohabitate, but who prefer a LAT-relationship.

I will now answer her questions, but as you continue reading, think about the kinds of questions that she did NOT ask.

#1 FOR THE 12% SINGLES AND 46% DIVORCED/WIDOWED WE DON'T KNOW IF THEY WANT TO COHABIT…

For well over a decade, I have been writing about the growing number of single people, mostly in the US but also around the world. When I mention, for example, that 103 million Americans, 18 and older, are divorced or widowed or have always been single, there has long been a predictable follow-up question: But aren't a lot of those cohabiting?

Not as many as you might think. When you subtract all of the cohabiting couples, including the same-sex couples, there are still 90 million Americans who are single and not cohabiting.

#2 UNLESS THEY KILLED THEIR HUSBANDS OR WIVES, WIDOW(ER)S CAN HARDLY BE CALLED SINGLES BY CHOICE...

When I first started studying single people and single life many years ago, there was one particular kind of story that really made an impression. It was told by people who had been widowed (usually women). One after another, they told me that they loved their husbands and that they had a good marriage. But, they added, they never wanted to marry again. No, they didn't kill their husbands, but now that they have experienced marriage, and are re-experiencing single life, they are CHOOSING single life.

#3 I SHOULD, OF COURSE, INCLUDE PEOPLE WHO DON'T WANT TO MARRY NOR COHABITATE, BUT WHO PREFER A LAT-RELATIONSHIP.

LAT means living apart together. It refers to couples who are committed to their relationship but do not want to share a home. Sometimes they are called dual dwelling duos. There is not a lot of research about this group, but the one estimate I found sets the number at about 6 or 7% of couples. My personal guess is that this trend is going to grow.

That's the end of the questions and my answers to them. So how did you do at generating the kinds of questions that were NOT asked? Here are a few of my own.

How many married people wish they were single? How many realize that getting married was a mistake, that for whatever reason they are not going to divorce, but if they ever did become single again, that's how they would stay?

How many single people, when asked if they want to marry, say yes, but then prioritize any actions that might increase the chance of that happening somewhere below cleaning out the sock drawer? Single people know that they are supposed to want to get married. That's the prevailing and unquestioned ideology of our time. Ask them on a survey and they will say, sure, I want to marry. Ask them informally yourself and maybe you will get the same answer. But what does it mean when they do not take any steps to try to make that happen?

How many single people think they want to get married because that's the only story of an adult life that they have ever heard, the only one they have seen celebrated on the big and small screen and in their everyday lives? How many single people would think differently about single life if all of the stereotyping and stigmatizing and getting ignored and excluded and getting discriminated against and all of the rest of the singlism simply did not exist?

What if single life were just as valid a choice as married or coupled life? How many single people would choose to be single then?

Imagine you were in living in the 1950s when the prevailing ideal for women was to stay home with the kids (and just about all of those women were married and had kids). Suppose that the claim, "my wife doesn't work," were a boast. Now do a survey. Ask those women—before the time of the *Feminine Mystique* and second-wave feminism—if they want to work. (It probably was done—if you know of it, please let me know.) How many would have said yes? Probably a very small number. Now transport those same women—with all the same genetic material—a half-century or so into the future. Now ask them if they want to work in paid employment. The difference from the 50s would be enormous.

We never know what people really would choose when only one choice is recognized and celebrated and the others are stereotyped and stigmatized. That's not a choice, it's ideology and culture. I don't know how many people would choose to be single if it were a valid, validated, and even celebrated choice in societies at large. But I bet my autographed Mickey Mantle baseball glove that the number would be higher than most people expect.

61.

Marriage Angst: Are Single People the Cause?

The answer to marriage angst you won't read anywhere else

October 30, 2011 by Bella DePaulo, Ph.D. at Psychology Today

There sure is a lot of marriage angst going around these days. Some of it is directed (projected?) by people who are married toward people who are not.

Ralph Richard Banks' provocatively titled book, Is Marriage for White People?, for instance, frets about all the single Black ladies, and urges them to consider marrying out of their race. Earlier, in his cover story in the NEW YORK TIMES MAGAZINE, "Married with Infidelities," Mark Oppenheimer suggested that with regard to adultery, "We are already a nation of forgivers...[and maybe] we should take some pride in that." Consider, too, *Marriage Confidential.* In that book, Pamela Haag explained her belief that marriage "needs to evolve to new forms." She is not just talking about a less inflexible attitude toward affairs but also more open-mindedness about asexuality and arrangements such as polyamory and living apart.

A few weeks ago, at the Huffington Post, Michele Willens asked this about women who are married:

> "Are you too hearing more and more women saying either: they need time and space to themselves; they are happy when their spouses are traveling; they are taking trips with other women or alone?"

Michele Willens asked me what I thought this was about, and after I sent her some thoughts, I kept thinking about her question. There are lots of possible answers, but here's my current favorite: Maybe single people are one of the causes of married people's angst.

That's not the way it is supposed to be. The National Marriage Project and all of the other purveyors of matrimania are busy trying to persuade singles that they will never be truly happy or complete or worthy unless they marry. Perhaps, though, people who actually are married are noticing something different: Single people, rather than sitting at home crying in their beer, are pursuing the life that is most meaningful to them. They are attending to the people who are important to them. They are pursuing their passions. They are settling into their own homes. (Single women are a major segment of the home-buying demographic.) They are creating the mix of time-with-others and time-to-themselves that best suits them.

Maybe that's what's got married people feeling so unsettled. They were supposed to be The Winners. They were supposed to be the ones who had it all, simply by virtue (and many do see it as a virtue) of having married. But with the number of unmarried Americans inching ever closer to the 50% mark - and we're not just talking young people, either - maybe married people can no longer remain oblivious to how the other half lives.

It is ironic, I think. Ask random persons in the street about the threat posed by single people to those who are married, and I bet their first threat to trip off their tongues is the sexual one. It is one of the most popular responses I get when I ask people why they think that couples socialize mostly with other couples. "Because the single person would try to steal someone's spouse," they say.

Maybe it is the married people who want to steal - not the single person, but the single person's life.

62.

Growing Fauxbivalence: Getting Married and Feeling Embarrassed about It

Hiding the signs of a marriage, and not to facilitate an affair

March 8, 2013 by Bella DePaulo, Ph.D at PsychCentral

I think the most powerful indication of the growing appeal of single life is what can't be faked – the numbers. For decades, every big new Census report has shown that the number and percentage of unmarried Americans is growing. (The trend is not specific to the U.S.)

Clearly, marriage is no longer obligatory and more and more people are choosing not to join The Married Couples Club.

Alongside those hard numbers are some intriguing stories of how some people who *do* choose to marry are feeling about their decision. Apparently, *they are embarrassed.* They want their engagement rings, but they don't want those rings to look too much like an engagement ring. The brides want the dress, but if it is white, they feel all apologetic about that. If they do the whole diet and workout routine before the wedding, they try to reframe their actions as not really about the wedding.

I don't know of any scientific study of this phenomenon yet, so what I am discussing here goes into the category of a trend story that may or may not be capturing an actual growing trend.

If this really is happening – even if the trend is a modest one, in size – I think it may be significant. Ideologically, it is a huge about-face from the matrimania I have been describing for well over a decade. Matrimania, the over-the-top hyping of weddings, coupling, and marriage, has long been practiced without any apology or self-consciousness. Couples, pundits, marriage-promoters, and of course, the Marriage Industrial Complex are delighted to peddle the belief that of course getting married is grand, that those who do walk down that path should feel proud and even superior to everyone else, and that the observers of the rings and the rituals should stop in their tracks to ooh and ahh (and contribute expensive gifts).

But is that changing?

Phoebe Maltz Bovy got me thinking about attitudes about marrying with her story in the *Atlantic*, "An ironic, low-key, unconventional wedding is still a wedding." The tag line: "An ethically sourced engagement ring doesn't change the fact that you're engaged, just like a girl who got her jewelry at Zales."

Bovy opens her article with a nod to the new engagement rings that do not look very traditional. They are rings, she believes, "for women happy to get married…but who would rather if the significance of said accessories be kept quiet."

The author coined the term "fauxbivalence":

> "Fauxbivalence is to be distinguished from cold feet, or a simple lack of interest in marriage. It refers exclusively to women who do want in on the institution, but who find this somehow embarrassing."

She adds: "The competitiveness one expects women to demonstrate regarding whose ring is flashiest lives on, only in the other direction."

Bovy believes that fauxbivalence may be especially intense among women who want not just marriage, but some of the conventional trappings of marriage. That, they believe, is *really* embarrassing!

The result of all this fauxbivalence, perhaps, is a spate of showy unconventionality. Hey look at my ring – it's ruby! It's ethically-sourced and uncut! It's plastic! But as Bovy notes, "the pressure to be different can be its own conformity."

Face it, the author tells the fauxbivalently engaged: No matter what jewelry you choose or what dress you wear, your wedding is not an expression of a new sentiment, and "you have not invented some radical new way for two human beings to relate to each other."

I like Phoebe Maltz Bovy's concluding piece of advice:

> "Rather than playing up the subtle distinction between your alternative, low-key wedding and that of a suburban princess, you might be an ally to those who don't wish to get married at all…"

Now, having positioned this fauxbivalence as a possible new trend, I want to walk that back a bit and suggest something different. That feeling has been around for a while. Maybe it comes and goes with prevailing cultural mores and conversations. In her book published back in 2001, *Here comes the bride: Women, weddings, and the marriage mystique*, Jaclyn Geller hilariously and insightfully critiqued all the 1990s attempts at off-beat weddings. She did not use the term fauxbivalence, but that – and more – was what she was describing.

63.

Is Marriage at 40 a Lateral Move?

Marrying at 40: his wife does not complete him

December 6, 2012 by Bella DePaulo, Ph.D at PsychCentral

If I had started writing a "single at heart" column in the 1950s, I would have had almost no natural audience. Hardly anyone stayed single through their 30s, much less for life, and there was little discussion of the joys of singlehood.

All that has steadily changed, decade by decade, and now year by year. The age at which people first marry – among those who do marry – continues to climb. More and more people stay single for life, and by choice.

Something new has hit the marital scene. Newlyweds who are in their 40s or 50s – and who are marrying FOR THE FIRST TIME – are no longer unheard of.

What happens when you are master of your own life for decades, and then you marry? I like answering questions with reams of data, but I also see the value of individual life stories. Over at Salon.com, Tim Gihring told his story of marrying at 40.

Titled I was a 'male spinster', the essay challenges some myths and swallows others whole. For example, Gihring does not like "the old trope that bachelors in their 40s are immature playboys who will never settle down, the floating scum of the dating pool." But he repeats uncritically claims such as the one about how marriage is likely to lengthen his lifespan. (I critiqued the relevant studies in SINGLED **OUT.**)

To me, the best parts of the essay were Gihring's discussions and analyses of his personal experiences of marrying at 40. Some highlights:

> I have a wife I love. But unlike people who marry at 22 or even 32, with some part of their adult experience still unformed, I have never thought that Lucy completes me. Or even that I'm happier than before. With no one to do it for me, I had already jury-rigged a life: a career, a circle of friends, a library card that I had every reason to

believe would sustain me to the end — and happily so. Marriage at 40 is a lateral move.

I'm reminded of this whenever Lucy and I fight, because our fights are not the fast-moving thunderstorms of youth but the daily drizzle of realizing you did all of this before on your own, from cooking to cleaning to driving cross-country, and never once criticized yourself. You never held up an ostensibly washed dish to yourself and said, "Do you see what I see?" You never asked yourself to roll up the windows, turn down the music, and watch the merging traffic until you sat there, tense in the silent car, thinking, "I knew road trips and you're no road trip."

64.

Clues that Marriage Might Not be Right for You

Conflict, cold feet, and other signs that marrying might be risky

October 19, 2012 by Bella DePaulo, Ph.D at PsychCentral

I love living single and I know that many other people do too, but that does not mean that it's for everyone. For some people, marriage may be the better option. But how can we know?

Of course, I think that most people who are single-at-heart live their most meaningful lives as single people. I don't have any data yet on how the lives of people who are single-at-heart change over time. For example, if people who are single-at-heart do marry, do they end up less happily married than those who are not single-at-heart? The relevant research has not yet been done.

The available research compares different kinds of couples to see which ones have happier or more lasting marriages. A study showing that cold feet (doubts about getting married) are a bad sign, especially for women, has already been discussed at PsychCentral. So in this post, I want to tell you about another study that adds to the evidence for the relevance of your own personal doubts, and adds another set of experiences that can also be warning signs.

In the research, 707 couples from Louisiana were surveyed within a few months of the wedding, then again about 21 months later and then about six years after the first contact. So the couples were followed for a total of about seven years, and the husbands and wives answered questions separately. (These were all hetero marriages.) Each time, the participants were asked how satisfied they were with their marriage overall, as well as with regard to love, physical intimacy, emotional intimacy, conflict resolution, fairness, quality of communication, and finances.

The question about cold feet asked participants whether they had been unsure about having made the right decision to marry "this person at this time."

The authors also believed that the following events, experienced before marrying, would be risk factors for less happy marriages:

- One person feels that he or she was not getting a "good picture" of what the other person was really like.

- The couple breaks up and gets together again more than once.

- There is a lot of conflict in the relationship.

- One or both partners was romantically or sexually involved with someone else at the same time

The wives and husbands were also asked about their beliefs about traditional sex roles. They indicated whether they agreed with statements such as the following:

- "All in all, family life suffers when the wife has a full-time job."

- "The husband should spend as much time as the wife taking care of infants and toddlers."

On the average, the couples became less and less satisfied with their marriages over time. The relevant question, then, is whether couples reporting the various risk factors became unhappier sooner than the couples without the risk factors.

The answer was yes. For both wives and husbands, pre-marital experiences of cold feet, not having a good picture of what the other person was really like, experiencing lots of conflict, multiple break-ups and involvement with others at the same time were all, on the average, bad news. People with those experiences had marriages that became unhappier sooner.

Traditional sex roles were also linked to LESS satisfying marriages. Remember that all of the couples were from Louisiana and about half of them were in covenant marriages.

There were two more factors that put couples at risk for becoming unhappier faster. One was having a preschool-aged child in the home. The other was being a woman. So on the average (meaning, the results are not true for every couple), married couples become less satisfied with their marriages over time, but the wives become dissatisfied sooner than the husbands do.

Reference:

DeMaris, A., Sanchez, L. A., & Krivickas, K. (2012). Developmental patterns in marital satisfaction: Another look at covenant marriage. JOURNAL OF MARRIAGE AND FAMILY, 74, 989-1004.

65.

The End of Marriage

Marriage has lost the biggest battle–control over our minds

June 16, 2014 by Bella DePaulo, Ph.D. at Psychology Today

Marriage is going down. I'm sure of it. Never again will it have the place of prominence that it once had in our lives.

Predicting the future is perilous. In the mid-1950s, marriage and nuclear family in the United States were at their peak. People got married younger than they had ever married before, they almost always had kids, and they stayed married (divorce was rare). When pundits and scholars and prognosticators were asked about the future of marriage and family, they predicted more of the same. No one saw the upheavals that were coming. It would have been utterly inconceivable to them that the future held a huge surge in the number of people staying single and living alone, along with big decreases in having children. No one predicted those things.

So how can I be so sure that marriage is going down?

There are solid reasons to think that the current trends are going to slow or even reverse. Can the proportion of single people continue to grow with each new Census Report? Is it even possible that the age at which people first marry–of those who do marry–will continue to climb? What about those millennials–will they be taken by nostalgia and start marrying sooner and more often than the generation before them?

All of this demographic slowing, and even some demographic reversals, are possible. They could happen. But I stand by my prediction: Marriage is going down.

It is going down in the more fundamental sense than mere numbers. Regardless of the numbers of people who do or do not marry, or how young or old they are when they do so, marriage is never going to be what it once was.

For women, marriage used to be economic life support. When there were fewer jobs open to women, and when those jobs paid even less than they do now, many women had to marry if they did not want to live in poverty. When attitudes were different, people had to marry in order to have sex without shame or stigma. They also had to marry in order to raise children without shame or stigma (though surely, some single-parent shaming persists). Now, with the pill and other forms of birth control, women can have sex without having children. Because of advances in reproductive science, they can also have kids without having sex. And they can do all of that outside of marriage.

None of that is ever going to change.

During these decades when the number of people staying single has been growing, when divorce has become commonplace, and when the age of first marriages is increasing, the millions of people without spouses have been innovating. They have been finding ways of living that suit them. Maybe they are living alone–lots of people are living alone. Maybe they are sharing a place with friends, not just as roommates splitting the rent but as housemates sharing a life. Maybe they have found a way to live close to friends or family while still maintaining a home of their own (some even keep their own homes even if they do marry–that's the "living apart together" or "dual-dwelling duos" phenomenon). Maybe they have created their own community, as has happened in more than 120 neighborhoods known as cohousing communities.

Some of these trends are very small. Added together, though, they are mighty. They are powerful enough to upend marriage and to topple to nuclear family.

What all of the choices and possibilities of contemporary life have really vanquished is a mindset. In the 1950s, it was obvious that there was one way that we should live our adult lives–as a couple, and then as a nuclear family. No one needed to write books with titles like "The Case for Marriage" because the case was self-evident. Even people who really did not fit into the mold of the heterosexual couple and nuclear family did not often make much of a fuss about it. They didn't realize that within the overwhelming numbers of people who got married and had kids were other people just like them– people who were doing that because that's what everyone else did, because that's what needed to be done to survive, because there were no models of other ways of living (or at least none that got much attention).

Marriage dominated not because it really was the best way to live for everyone, but because it was uncontested. No, it was even more extreme than that–hardly anyone even thought to try to contest it.

That's over.

Even if more people get married tomorrow than they did today, even if next year, people start marrying at younger ages than they did last year, marriage will never be the same.

Marriage was once the only way to live. It was, we thought, the only truly good and moral and deeply rewarding way to journey through life.

That's over. That is so over. That marriage is dead.

About the Author

Bella DePaulo (Ph.D., Harvard University) writes myth-busting, consciousness-raising, totally unapologetic books on single life. The *Atlantic* magazine has described her as "America's foremost thinker and writer on the single experience."

Dr. DePaulo's books get much attention because of her expertise, her high profile in the media, and her years of writing for popular audiences. Her work has been described in the most influential newspapers, including *New York Times* (many times), the *Washington Post*, the *Wall Street Journal*, and *USA Today*, and in widely-read magazines such as the *New Yorker*, *Time*, *AARP Magazine*, *Newsweek / The Daily Beast*, the *Week*, the *Economist*, *More*, *Glamour*, *Cosmopolitan*, *Elle*, *Readers' Digest*, *Prevention*, the *Nation*, *Business Week*, *US News & World Report*, *Realtor Magazine*, the *Chronicle of Higher Education*, and the *Atlantic*. Many newspapers and magazines around the world have also discussed her ideas. Bella DePaulo has been writing the "Living Single" blog for *Psychology Today* since 2008. She also blogs for PsychCentral and has contributed to the Huffington Post. She has appeared many times on radio and television.

Dr. DePaulo, who is also an expert on the psychology of deceiving and detecting deceit, has lectured nationally and internationally. She has given workshops and has addressed criminal attorneys, judges, polygraphers, members of the national intelligence community (such as the CIA and the FBI), physicists, marketing professionals, high school teachers, and medical and mental health practitioners. She has been invited to speak at think tanks, government agencies, political meetings, singles advocacy groups, literary conferences, book clubs, book festivals, women's centers, newcomers groups, and many universities.

Bella DePaulo is the winner of the Excellence in Research Award, bestowed by the American Association for Single People. The author of more than 100 scholarly publications, including more than a dozen books, she has also won two prestigious academic awards, the Research Scientist Development Award and the James McKeen Cattell Award. Professor DePaulo has served in leadership positions in professional organizations and has served on the editorial boards of many journals. She is currently a Project Scientist in the psychology department at the University of California at Santa Barbara. Visit Dr. DePaulo's website at www.BellaDePaulo.com.

Printed in Great Britain
by Amazon

19881751R00108